9/15

# CARD & MAGIC TRICKS

OVER 30 EASY-TO-PERFORM STUNTS TO AMAZE AND CONFOUND

EVE DEVEREUX AND PETER ELDIN

**GRAMERCY BOOKS**

**NEW YORK**

This 2004 edition is published by Gramercy Books, an imprint of Random House Value
Publishing, a division of Random House, Inc., New York, by arrangement with Quantum
Publishing Limited, London.

Gramercy is a registered trademark and the colophon is a trademark of
Random House, Inc.

Random House
New York • Toronto • London • Sydney • Auckland
www.randomhouse.com

QUMCMT

This book is Produced by
Quantum Publishing
6 Blundell Street
London  N7 9BH

Manufactured in Singapore by
Pica Digital Pte Ltd
Printed in Singapore by
Star Standard Industries Pte Ltd

A catalog record for this title is available from the Library of Congress.

ISBN 0-517-22309-0

10 9 8 7 6 5 4 3 2 1

# CONTENTS

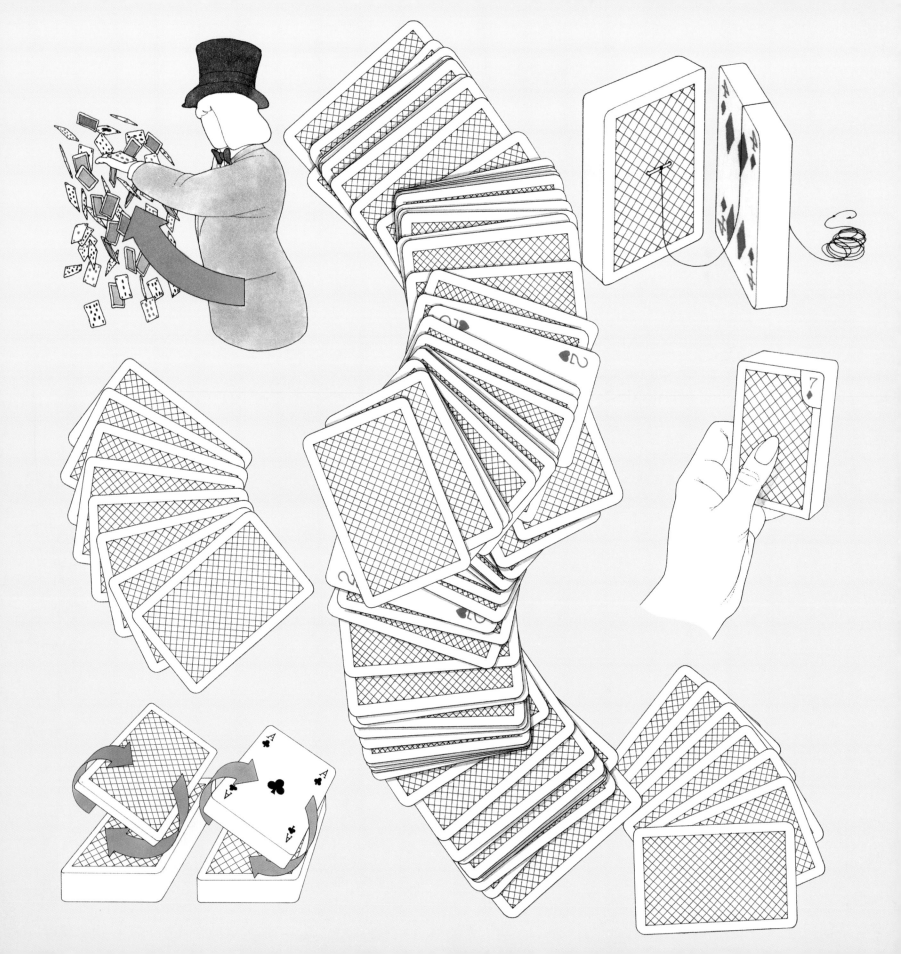

# CARD
# TRICKS

EVE DEVEREUX

# INTRODUCTION

No book can teach you how to be a magician: it can only teach you how to perform tricks. The rest is entirely up to you.

This is because performance magic – conjuring – is really one great big con trick, with the performer being only one of the con artists involved. The audience know that you are not using real magic, that you are cheating them in some way, yet they are prepared to maintain the fiction in their own minds that you are using abilities that have not been granted to the mass of humankind. At least, they are prepared to maintain this fiction so long as you present your con tricks with sufficient charm (or, rarely, anti-charm) and vivacity to persuade the audience that you are keeping to your side of the unwritten bargain – that you are working very hard to keep them entertained. Successful criminal con artists have almost always relied on this: they work with such charm and ingenuity that their dupes *want* to believe in them!

## PATTER

This is your major aid, especially when performing a routine consisting entirely or largely of card tricks. Cards do not (usually) jump through hoops or burst into flames, or any of the other things that more elaborate magical props can be called upon to do: they are merely immobile pieces of pasteboard, although often enough you will be trying to persuade your audience that they are anything but. Instead, therefore, you must arrange for all the ostentatious magical effects to take place inside your audience's heads: you must manipulate their minds – indeed, that is exactly what they want you to do.

Your best tool for doing this is patter, which is also your main ally in directing the audience's attention away from things you do not wish them to notice (misdirection). Every card trick can be made to tell a story, and ideally it should be a story that you have invented yourself. Indications of the type of yarns you might tell are given in this book. Many tricks (eg, the scurvy Knaves tricks – see pages 34–35) have traditionally had such tales attached to them. Best of all, though, is if you take the basis of a trick, adapt it as you want, and then invent your own story to go along with it.

Also an important part of your patter is the relationship you establish with the audience. Usually you will want to make them laugh, to get them on your side; you can even get them on your side by consistently insulting them, just as long as your insults are witty enough. However, do not be tempted to make humiliating jokes at the expense of those members of the audience you ask to help you (in this book always called volunteers). The volunteers have paid their entrance money just like everyone else, and may have conquered considerable nervousness to assist you in front of a hall of spectators, so to hurt their feelings would be unforgivably discourteous.

Work on building up the sequence of tricks you want to perform to make a full routine. One line of patter should not end at the finish of one trick, to be replaced by a quite different line at the start of the next. All through the routine, the various elements of your patter should flow naturally into one another. Deciding on a theme is a good way of doing this; a running joke can be helpful.

## YOU

For the purposes of clarity, throughout this book it has been assumed that the magician is female and that all the volunteers from the audience are male; in the very few tricks where an accomplice is required, again the assumption is femaleness.

It has also been assumed that the magician is right-handed, but on the rare occasions where the directions might be confusing to a left-hander the text indicates as much.

Your choice of dress onstage is something that you will evolve for yourself – you will probably dress differently for different occasions. For most tricks it does not matter what you wear; but some require pockets or specific garments. Again for the sake of simplicity, this book assumes that you will wear trousers (not tight ones, like jeans) with standard pockets, an opaque shirt (preferably) or blouse, and a jacket with side and top (breast) pocket. One trick requires you to be carrying a handkerchief: this should be large, opaque, clean, and freshly ironed. The best way to carry it, unless it would clash entirely with the rest of your presentation, is formally folded in one of the top pockets of your jacket.

## PROPS, GIMMICKS AND ACCOMPLICES

The tricks in this book can be done by a solitary performer using standard cards: they can be done anywhere.

For many performances, however, it is desirable to have onstage with you a table and a couple of chairs. For your table, a simple folding card-table is perfectly adequate. If you put a tablecloth on it, do not use one that drapes generously to the floor on all sides – that would immediately convince your audience that the table was rigged with all sorts of cunning gadgets and gimmicks, and they would become suspicious every time you approached it. A thin, small tablecloth, of an area about the same as the tabletop but set crosswise on it so that the corners hang, is perfectly sufficient. You might think of using a patterned tablecloth, since on occasion you will indeed be dropping or picking up things that the audience should know nothing about; for the same reason, it is wise if there are a few bits of "clutter" on the table – empty card-boxes, perhaps even a vase of flowers.

The chairs are useful because, especially in intimate venues, many card tricks are best performed when both you and a volunteer are seated on either side of your table.

Be careful when employing an accomplice. In very many cases the relationship between you and your accomplice will be either immediately guessed or already known.

Gimmicks and gadgets can likewise bring down your performance, especially if almost every trick you do relies on them: you know better than anyone else that your assumed cleverness is a complete sham, and this awareness is likely to communicate itself to the audience. Use such artifices sparingly. For your interest, however, a trick has been included here (Hopscotch from the Deck – see pages 46–47) which requires a fairly complicated gadget. Try it – you may find that you are one of those people who actually prefer gadget-oriented magic.

## THE CARDS THEMSELVES

Doctored cards – with extra-rounded corners, or with their edges shaved – are another matter: a number of very fine tricks can be done using cards treated in this way, and you will find them (and basic instructions on how to do the doctoring) in some of the tricks in this book. On a few occasions, fake or dummy cards can be useful too.

For the most part, however, all you need is a single deck of cards – although preferably you should possess two decks, with matching fronts but different back-designs. Buy the best-quality cards you can reasonably afford: cheap ones are a complete waste of money. Your cards should have a plastic finish, both for durability and so that their surfaces glide easily over each other. It is handy to have an extra deck identical in all respects to one of your two main decks, but with a textured "linen" finish rather than a smooth one.

When one or both of your decks get scruffy through overuse, replace the pair. Do not throw away your old decks, though. Not only can they be useful for practice (better, often, than nice clean new ones), you can cannibalize them for use in making fakes, to replace cards accidentally destroyed, or simply to have an extra copy of a particular card to use in a trick.

Buy cards whose back-designs include a white margin all the way around. Often enough you will want to persuade a volunteer that you are offering him a face-down deck when in fact it is a face-up deck with its topmost card turned face-down. A white margin allows you to splay the deck a little to aid the deception.

Specially faked cards can be bought from conjuring shops, and on occasion they can be useful, though most often you are better off manufacturing your own. For larger venues you might think of buying Jumbo Cards (also known as

Giant Cards), but these are extremely expensive and can be used for only a limited repertoire of tricks – imagine trying to shuffle a deck of Jumbo Cards!

One other special type is worth considering. If your hands are small, you may find it difficult to do many of these tricks using a standard deck. Try them again using a deck of solitaire (patience) cards. These little cards are generally very attractive, largely just because of their smallness, and you could make the fact that you use them a distinctive and appealing feature of your act.

## PRACTICE!

It is an old adage of magic that you should practice any trick until you know it thoroughly, then until you can do it every time perfectly without even thinking about it, and then a bit more so that you can do it better than that!

LEFT: The Riffle Shuffle (see page 10). Once mastered, this shuffle is both efficient and impressive. It will add a hint of professionalism to your routine.

# BASIC TECHNIQUES

## STRAIGHT SHUFFLE

This is the shuffle that most of us ordinarily use when playing cards. It is open to various deceptions, for all of which you should have the basic shuffle sufficiently practiced that you can do it very quickly and easily and that no one watching can really keep track of the cards.

The deck starts in the left hand, with the cards facing towards the inside of the hand (i.e., towards the ball of the thumb). The fingers and thumb of the right hand grip the ends of most of the deck, lifting it up so that a small packet remains in the left hand.

The right hand then drops a few cards into the left on the inside of this packet, then a few to its outside, then a few on the inside, and so on until all the cards are once more in the left hand.

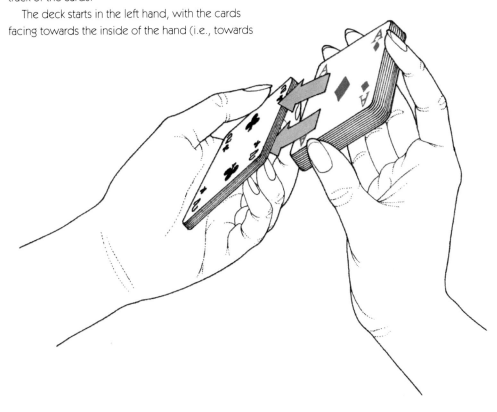

# STRAIGHT-SHUFFLE DECEPTIONS

The straight shuffle is more open to simple fakery than most other types of shuffle.

♣ It is easy to keep the original top card of the deck at the top. You simply ensure that the final few cards are dropped from the right hand always to the rear of the packet in the left hand. Similarly, you can keep several cards at the top of the deck, in order – up to as many as 15 or even 20.

♣♣ You can likewise keep the deck's bottom card or cards at the bottom. Merely start the shuffle with the cards facing not inwards towards the ball of the left hand's thumb, but outwards, facing away from it.

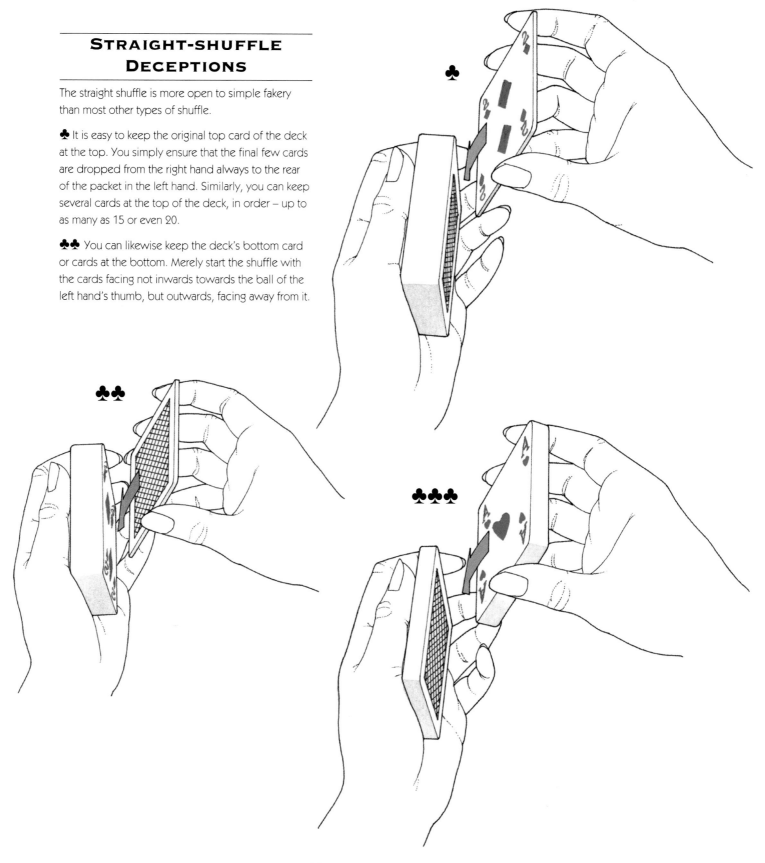

♣♣ You can, in fact, not shuffle the cards at all. Although you go through all the motions of an ordinary shuffle, you consistently drop the cards from the right hand *behind* the growing packet in the left hand. You cannot hope to get away with this every time if you perform the maneuver directly in front of the audience, but it can be handy to know you can do it while turning away or while diverting the audience's attention elsewhere – simply to add to the illusion that you really are shuffling the cards thoroughly.

♣♣♣ You can shuffle a card from the bottom of the deck to the top. In your first pick-up with the right hand, leave only a single card in the left. For a preliminary shuffle, always drop the cards on the inside of the growing packet in the left hand. Immediately start a second shuffle, to disguise the paucity of this first one, this time shuffling normally except retaining the new top card in place.

♣♣♣♣ You can shuffle a card from the center of the deck to the top, assuming that you have located the card through having made a break in the deck (perhaps with a fingernail). Here the first packet you pick up with the right hand contains all the cards down to the break (not including the chosen card). Your procedure is then as in the previous shuffle.

♣♣♣♣♣ You can use a shuffle to arrange that there is a face-up card at the bottom of a face-down deck. First, at the end of an orthodox shuffle, wrap the fingers of the left hand around the deck to grip the last card. Then pick up the rest of the deck with the right hand, and at once seemingly use both hands simply to square up the deck.

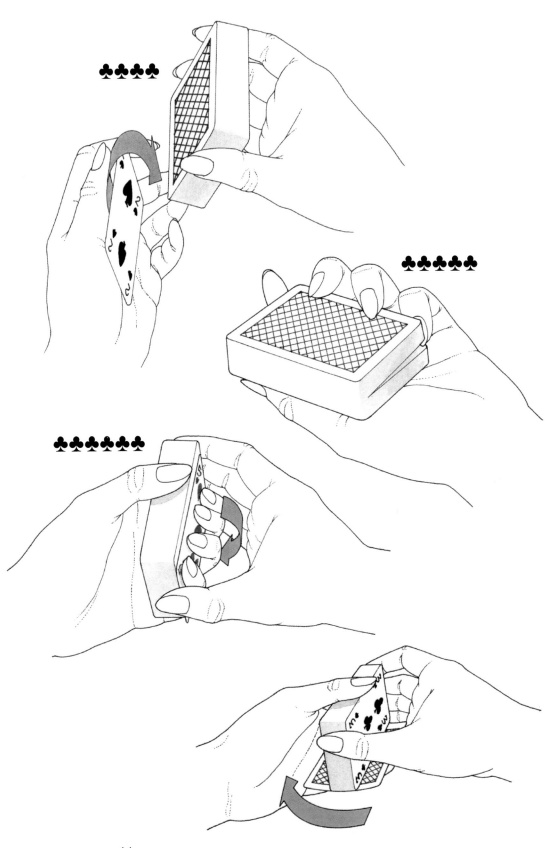

## RIFFLE SHUFFLE

The riffle shuffle is another that is frequently used when playing card games.

♥ You cut the deck into two packets, place both face-down on a flat surface with their corners adjacent, bend the corners up with the thumbs, move the two packets still closer together, and release the cards such that the corners of the two packets interlock with a satisfying riffling sound. You can then use both hands to merge the two packets, so that the deck is restored with its cards thoroughly rearranged. Alternatively, you can make the shorter edges of the two packets overlap, rather than just the corners. This variant is often called the dovetail shuffle.

♥♥ Rather more difficult is the riffle shuffle performed without recourse to a flat surface. The two packets face towards each other as you start, one in each hand, the cards being held between the thumbs and the first joints of the fingers. Bring

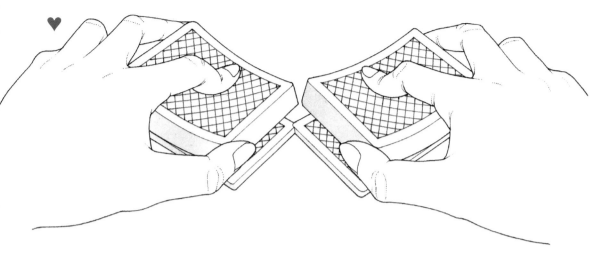

the index finger of each hand around and press its back against the rear of the respective packet; then bring the thumbs closer together and riffle the ends of the cards into each other. You may require a good deal of practice to master this – and you may not consider the practice worth it, since the two simpler techniques look better.

## PALMING

Palming makes it possible for you to have cards in your hand when the audience believes your hands to be empty. There are two principal techniques.

### TECHNIQUE 1

♠ A card can be held on the inside of the hand, curved into the palm and braced, usually, between the ball of the thumb and the second joints of the fingers. People with big hands will have the upper edge of the card braced against the second joints of all four fingers (or even against the base of the fingers); those with smaller hands can brace it against the second joints of the three fingers other than the index finger. If your hands are very small, try the exercise using a solitaire (patience) card: you may find it better to use such cards for all tricks that require palming. Now practice palming the top card from the deck so easily that it looks as if your hand has merely glided over the surface. You might also try palming more than one card at a time.

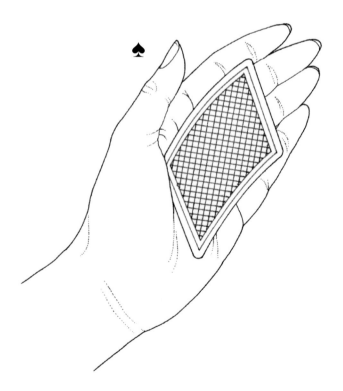

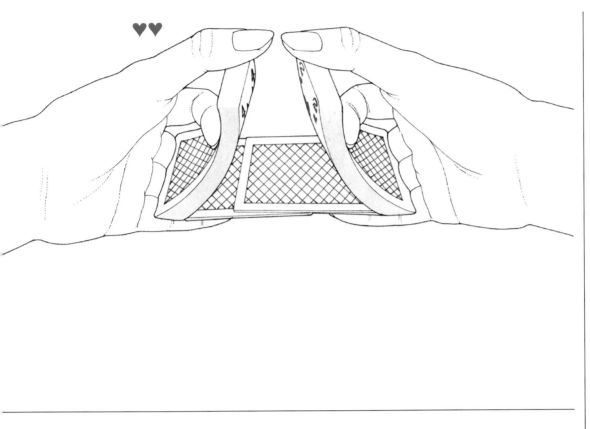

♥ ♥

## HINDOO SHUFFLE

The Hindoo Shuffle looks slick and allows deceptions that are not possible with other shuffles. It is rarely used in playing card games, but is more widely employed by magicians, since it requires a lot of practice.

At the start, the deck is held horizontally face-down by the fingers and thumb of the right hand. Advance the deck toward the cupped left hand, and grip the top cards of the deck between its fingers and thumb, with the index finger moved around the end of the received deck for purposes of control (if it is not there, you are soon going to be throwing cards all over the floor – enough of a danger anyway when learning the shuffle.) The right hand takes the bulk of the deck away from beneath this top packet, which you let fall from the left hand's fingers towards the cupped palm as the right hand advances the deck to repeat the process.

As noted, a well-executed Hindoo shuffle looks slick, because it is *obviously* a difficult maneuver. For that same reason, no one will be surprised if the amassed cards in your left hand look a bit sloppy. This leaves the way open for one of the deceptions possible with this shuffle. At any stage during the shuffle you can irritably use the cards still remaining in the right hand to tap those in the left into better order, and this gives you the opportunity to glimpse the bottom card of the packet in the right hand. It is clearly simple thereafter to make sure that this card becomes the top card in the deck when the shuffle is completed.

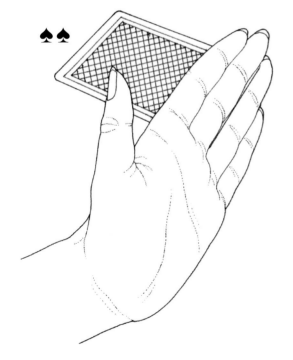

♠ ♠

### TECHNIQUE 2

♠ ♠ This allows you to display the open face of your hand to the audience, showing it to be empty, when in fact you are holding a card. The card is held, by one of its short ends, between the second and third fingers and almost all of it sticks out at the back of the hand; the thin edge of card does not show between the fingers, either because of the line between them already naturally there or because their flesh touches in front of the card's edge, obscuring it. It is not at all difficult to hold cards in this way – what is difficult is actually getting them there in the first place. None of the tricks in this book use this palming technique, which is included here solely for the sake of completeness: the most likely result of your attempting to use it is that you drop or show the card at the most embarrassing possible moment, thereby destroying the effect of the trick.

# THE PASS

The object of the pass is to bring a card to the top or bottom of the deck unknown to the audience. Typically you will have asked a volunteer to pick a card and then returned it to the center of the proffered deck. There are two common methods whereby you can then immediately bring that card to the top.

Try adapting both of these techniques – particularly Technique 1 – so that you can allow volunteers to return their cards to a fanned deck.

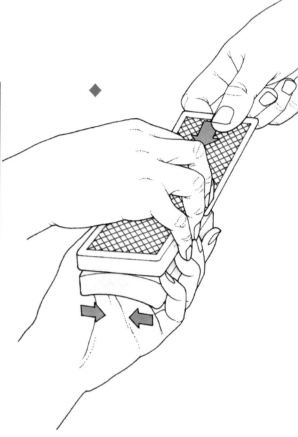

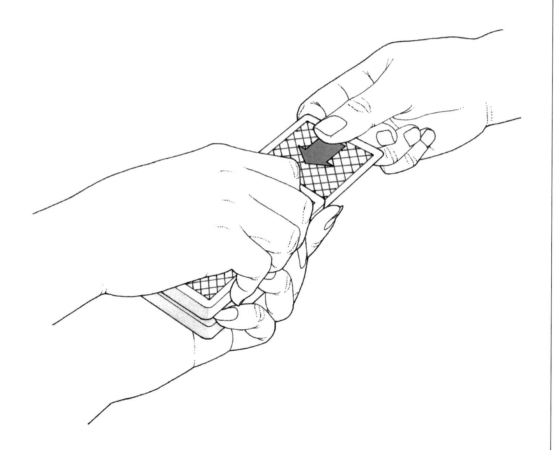

## TECHNIQUE 2

You must be prepared to put in a lot of practice if you are to get this technique right, so that you can perform it smoothly and quickly enough for it to be undetectable to the volunteer, who is probably still close in front of you. You should also practice it for transferring just a single card from the bottom to the top of the deck – this is perhaps its most useful application. Don't be discouraged if you keep dropping the cards all over the floor in your early attempts: most people do. Your aim is to become so accustomed to the maneuver that it is almost instinctive, so practice on boring train journeys or anywhere else that you have time – and cards – on your hands. If your hands are big enough, you may find that you can eventually execute the Pass one-handed.

◆ As the card is inserted, the fingers of your left hand, holding the deck, should crimp the sides of the packet beneath that card, putting a slight bend on those cards, so that the two packets become quite distinct from each other.

◆◆ The middle fingers of your left hand can then reach across the top of the deck to pull the upper packet sideways away from the lower.

## TECHNIQUE 1

This involves your having at least one long fingernail on the hand in which you hold the deck, preferably on the little finger of the left hand. Although the volunteer thinks he is putting the selected card back into a random place in the deck, in fact, hidden from his view by the cards, you have already inserted your fingernail into the deck's rear corner,

splitting it into two packets. As you offer the deck to him with both your hands, it is easy with the right hand to displace the two packets just a trifle sideways from each other as he is pushing his card towards it. The card in place, swiftly begin to give the deck a straight shuffle, beginning by cutting the deck at the position of your fingernail so that the selected card is brought to the top.

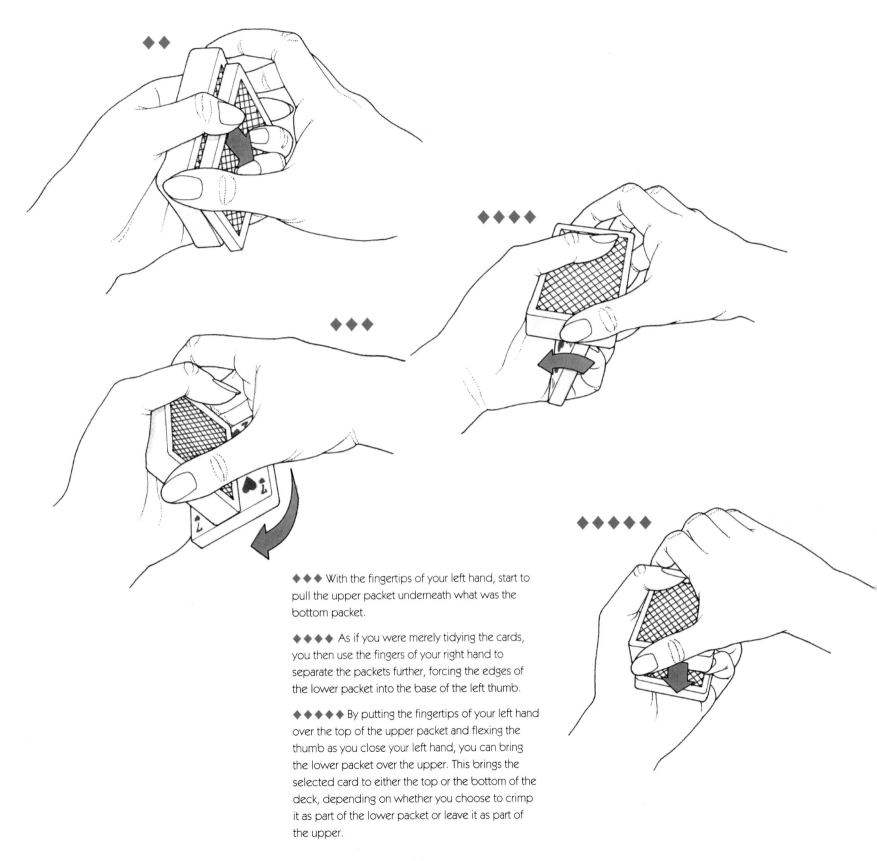

◆◆◆ With the fingertips of your left hand, start to pull the upper packet underneath what was the bottom packet.

◆◆◆◆ As if you were merely tidying the cards, you then use the fingers of your right hand to separate the packets further, forcing the edges of the lower packet into the base of the left thumb.

◆◆◆◆◆ By putting the fingertips of your left hand over the top of the upper packet and flexing the thumb as you close your left hand, you can bring the lower packet over the upper. This brings the selected card to either the top or the bottom of the deck, depending on whether you choose to crimp it as part of the lower packet or leave it as part of the upper.

## FORCING A CARD

The object of all techniques of forcing cards is to make a volunteer think that he has selected a card at random, whereas, in fact, the one that he has chosen has been predetermined by you.

The simplest method of forcing is also the most fallible, and you should use it only when you are certain of your audience; ideally, they should be casual and laughing, already convinced by other tricks that you are more or less infallible – even better if you are performing at a party or in a bar, so that everyone has had a few drinks.

While fanning out the deck or immediately afterwards, edge forward a little with your thumbnail or thumb the predetermined card – which should be roughly in the center of those that you have fanned out. (Note that, in fanning out a complete deck, you need only proffer the central cards of the deck with the others to either side being more bunched up.)

A casual volunteer will probably choose the card that is protruding slightly from the rest; if not, it is easy enough casually to rotate your wrists a little to bring the predetermined card gradually under his descending fingers.

If still unsuccessful, suddenly "remember" some part of the trick you have forgotten to set up, and retreat to your table. Either try this technique of forcing on a different member of the audience, or, preferably, use one of the alternatives described on these two pages.

### THE BRIDGE

Your predetermined card is at the bottom of the deck. Cut the deck yourself first, crimping the (original) upper packet as you do so to form a bridge. As you complete the cut, therefore, there will be a distinct gap between the upper and lower packets.

Offer the deck in your hand to the volunteer and ask him to cut the deck. If you do this quickly and offhandedly enough, he will invariably cut at the gap, and thereby at your predetermined card.

You can do this at your table rather than offering the deck in your hand. However, this is much more risky. Not only are you giving the volunteer much more time to think, and hence to cut at somewhere other than the obvious place, but also you are not in control of which way he habitually takes the cards when cutting a deck – most people grip the cards at the sides but some grip them at the

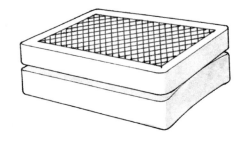

ends – and consequently you may have crimped the bridge in the wrong direction – widthways when it should have been lengthways, or vice versa. By offering the cards in your hand you determine the way the volunteer cuts the deck, whatever his normal practice.

### CUT IT YOURSELF

This is a very simple way of forcing either one or a pair of cards on a volunteer. Ask him to cut the deck wherever he wants, and then either you or he can lay the ex-bottom half of the deck crosswise over the top. Because of his participation, the volunteer believes the two crossed cards at the new center of the deck have been randomly selected; in fact, of course, they are the cards that were originally at the top and bottom of the deck.

Perform this force quickly and with the maximum of distracting patter.

## DEAL IT YOURSELF

The predetermined card is at the top of the deck. To show that the selection process is truly random, keep shuffling the deck, ensuring that you retain the predetermined card in its place, while asking the volunteer to think of any number between 1 and 52.

When he has done so, stop shuffling, and tell him you want him to count off the cards from the top of the deck until he reaches that number – demonstrate this yourself to make it absolutely clear

what you want him to do: if his number was 17, count off 16 cards and show him the 17th (which is, of course, of no interest). Put the 17th card on top of the heap you have counted off and then return this heap to the top of the deck.

Pass the deck to him and ask him to repeat the exercise. Obviously, because of your "demonstration," the card that started at the top of the deck is now the 17th down from the top.

## THE RIFFLE FORCE

♣ The predetermined card is at the top of the deck. Holding the deck face-down in your right hand, with your fingers wrapped around it, riffle one corner of the exposed end with your thumb. Do this a few times through the deck, and then ask the volunteer to stop you at any time mid-riffle. When he does so, reach across with your left hand and remove the cards of the upper packet, offering him the lower packet, the top card of which is the one his call has selected.

♣♣ In fact, when drawing the upper packet away from the lower, the tips of the wrapped-around fingers of your right hand have pressed against the back of the top card so that, as you drew the packet away, that card stayed in your right hand and fell naturally onto the lower packet. With a little rehearsal you will find you can perform the whole maneuver so swiftly and naturally that it is undetectable.

In practice, the right hand's fingertips often retain two or three cards rather than just the top one, but of course this does not matter – and with practice you can use this to your advantage in order to force more than one card simultaneously.

## SHUFFLE-STOP

The predetermined card can start either at the top or at the bottom of your deck. You tell the volunteer that you want him to call out at any moment while you are shuffling. The shuffle you perform looks like a normal straight shuffle (see page 9), but in fact it is a close variant. If the predetermined card has started at the top of the deck, perform a straight shuffle to take it to the bottom.

For the variant shuffle you use from here on, pick off a packet not from the outside of the deck but from the inside (i.e., from the side of the deck closer to the ball of your thumb). The cards you then drop to either side of the new central cluster come in groups from the rear, not the front, of this packet, so that the bottom few cards of the packet are retained firmly between your fingertips until, at last, you drop them at the bottom of the deck.

Repeat this over and over while telling the volunteer what you want him to do. Whatever time he calls out to you to stop, the face-out card at the bottom of the packet in your upper hand will always be the one you selected in advance.

Practice this variant of the straight shuffle: it is much easier than it sounds. It can be tricky with new cards or with excessively old and greasy ones, so use a worn deck both in practice and for the performance.

## FLYING CARDS

With the flying cards maneuver, the magician is able to throw a card, accurately and quickly, to a member of the audience. In fact, she is able to do this several times in quick succession, each time to a different member of the audience.

This is an embellishment that you can use at any stage of your performance. There is no deception involved: merely the acquisition of the knack.

### TECHNIQUE 1

♥ Hold the card with one of its shorter edges between the first and second fingers of your hand.

♥♥ To throw it, you extend your arm suddenly while at the same time giving the card a backward flick out of your fingers so that it skims horizontally through the air; the movement as a whole is much the same as if you were hitting a backhand shot in table tennis. The first few times you try this, the card will merely flutter in the air in front of you, but sooner or later – it may be on your third attempt, it may not come for half an hour – you will suddenly find that you manage to throw the card perfectly. Practice for a little longer and you'll be able to get it right every time.

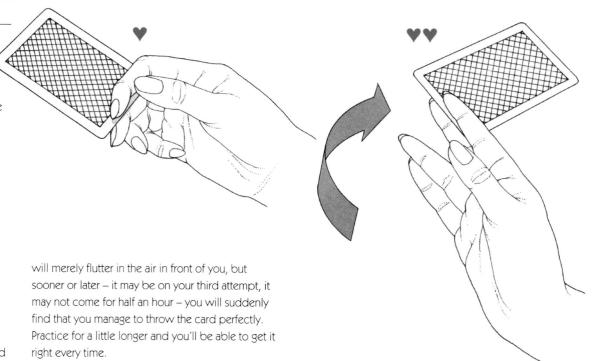

### TECHNIQUE 2

A card is selected in the customary way, and then returned to the deck. The magician starts throwing cards towards the audience, to show that she is performing with a perfectly standard deck; apparently to the surprise of the magician as much as anyone else, one card pauses over the heads of the audience and comes back to her. This proves to be the chosen card.

The method is as follows. Use either of the passes (see pages 14–15) and a straight shuffle (see page 9) to get the selected card to the bottom of the deck. Throw the first few cards from the top of the deck using the technique outlined for the previous trick. Once you feel you have done this enough, choose as your next card the one from the bottom (i.e., the selected card). This you must grip a little differently.

♠ Hold the near corner of one of its shorter sides between your thumb and all fingertips except that of the index finger; the index fingertip rests on the corner further away from you.

♠♠ Your throw this time is not horizontal but upward at an angle of about 45 degrees; moreover, you throw more gently. As you release the card, give it a flick with the index fingertip. When the card reaches the top of its arc it will come spinning back towards you.

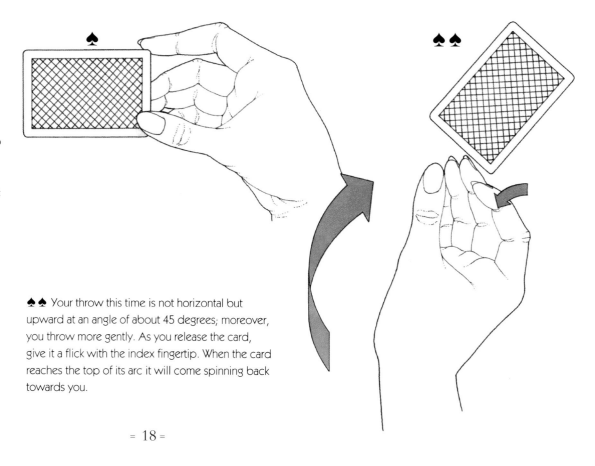

## TECHNIQUE 3

This technique begins with the magician asking a volunteer to choose a card, which is then returned to the deck. While it is being shown around in the usual way, the magician explains how playing cards have often reminded her of pigeons, except that – for the obvious reason that cards have no brains at all – it is more difficult to teach them to come "home." She encourages the volunteer and his friends to inculcate the principle into the chosen card by singing to it a piece of doggerel – e.g., "You're the cleverest playing card in the pack, so show us you are by flying right back." After they have made fools of themselves for long enough, the card is returned to the deck, which the magician shuffles. She then throws the deck in the air so that the cards flutter down around her. As they clear, a single card is seen to be sitting on the back of her still outstretched hand, and this proves to be the card that was taught.

To make this work, while the volunteer and his friends are drawing the attention of the rest of the audience, you touch the back of your right hand to a blob of something sticky (honey) that you put on your table beforehand. As soon as the card is returned to the deck, make the pass (see pages 12–13) to bring it to the top.

◆ During the process of turning to throw the cards upwards, find the opportunity to press the sticky back of your hand to the back of the chosen card. With your hand turned so that its back is away from the spectators, throw the rest of the deck in the air.

◆◆ In the confusion of the falling cards, simply turn your hand to reveal the card. Make sure of your timing. If you turn your hand too soon or too late, the audience will see what is going on.

Because of the stickiness, you should either make this the last trick of your routine or switch decks before the next trick.

Alternatively, it is possible to do without the honey:

♣ After you have passed the card to the top of the deck, secure it between your first and second fingers.

♣♣ Very quickly move to throw the cards up, simultaneously using your thumb to push the selected card back between the fingers, so that it protrudes to the rear of your hand. Then, as the cards fall all around your outstretched hand, make a lunge with it (as if trying to catch something) and turn it so that the card is revealed.

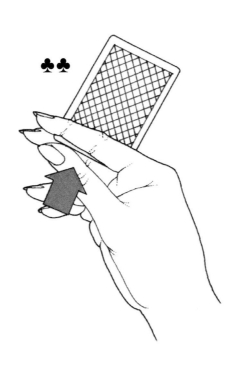

# CARDS THAT SPELL

◆

## Convince your audience that you have taught your cards to spell!

### TRICK 1

The magician asks a volunteer to select a card at random from the deck and show it, explaining that she has succeeded in teaching the cards in this particular deck how to spell – well, at least their own names. On the card being returned to the deck, she shuffles and then asks the volunteer to count down from the top of the deck, peeling off one card for each letter of the card he chooses – e.g., T-H-R-E-E O-F C-L-U-B-S. At the end of this exercise, it is found to the magician's dismay that the card turned up is not in fact the Three of Clubs. She asks the volunteer to spell out his card again, and this time it shows up as the final "s" of "Clubs."

1 Have a volunteer pick a card. Using the pass (see pages 14–15) in the normal way, bring the card to the top of the deck. The card turned up will be the wrong card.

2 Explain angrily that these cards are a bit thick, put the discarded heap back on the top of the deck and shout at the deck as a whole. From here on the trick works itself. Because the chosen card is at the bottom of the packet you return to the top of the deck, the second attempt will be successful.

### TIP

• When the first attempt proves a failure, you can initially blame the volunteer, accusing him of having been unable himself to spell the card's name correctly. The byplay will distract the audience from thinking about the fact that the card spelled out the second time must inevitably be the one that was at the top of the deck earlier. You can then ask him to "prove" himself by doing the deal for you. This trick should not be performed more than once in your routine, but you can follow it up with the next trick.

### TRICK 2

The magician announces that she has taught the cards in the deck to spell their own names. She asks a volunteer to draw a card from the deck, to tell her what it is, to return it, and to shuffle the deck as much as he wishes; she then explains that, if she spells the name of the card down from the top of the deck, removing one card for each letter of the chosen card's name – e.g., T-H-R-E-E O-F C-L-U-B-S – the final card turned up will indeed be the Three of Clubs. To show that there is no deception, she will perform the exercise blindfolded – indeed, to make doubly sure, she will even put the deck in her pocket and count from there. Blindfolded, she spells out the cards from the pocket and the final "S" does indeed correspond to the Three of Clubs.

1 Before the trick, secrete a duplicate deck in your pocket, sorted into suit and rank order; furthermore, divide the suits off from each other with pieces of card just a little bigger than the cards.

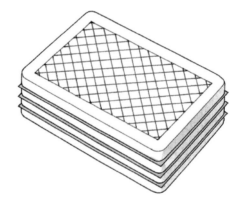

2 Put the displayed deck in your pocket while you are asking a volunteer to blindfold you, to make sure the blindfold is secure, etc. During this time it will seem quite natural that your hand remains in the pocket, and the physical activity of the blindfolding will disguise any movement your arm makes as you pick out the correct card from the duplicate deck.

3 You then spell out random cards from the "real" deck through T-H-R-E-E O-F C-L-U-B and produce the duplicate Three of Clubs itself for the final "S."

### TIPS

• It may seem obvious, but remember that you should not set down the earlier cards of the spelling face-up – there's a reasonable chance that one of them will be the "real" Three of Clubs!
• This trick is an ideal follow-up to the previous one, in which the cards of the deck "get it wrong" the first time the exercise is tried. It seems natural to explain that, this time, you will put the chosen card to the sterner test of being able to spell its name in the dark.
• This trick can, in turn, be followed by a very swift execution of the next one.

## TRICK 3

The magician sorts out all the cards of one suit (e.g., Spades) from the deck, and puts the rest of the cards to one side. She then explains that the Spades are the cleverest of the suits, and that each of them can spell its own name. She starts spelling them off from the top of the packet with A-C-E, putting each of the first two cards to the bottom of the packet and turning up the Ace to correspond to the "E." Putting the Ace to one side, she continues to spell T-W-O, and the Two is turned up with the "O," and discarded. She continues right through until the final card left in her hands is the King.

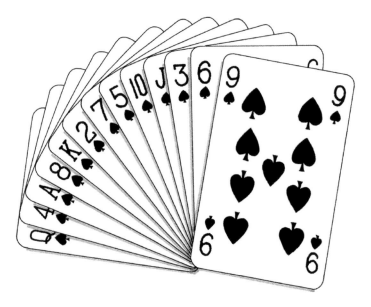

1 As you are sorting out the Spades from the rest, scatter them fairly widely over your table. This will make it less obvious that you are not picking them up again at random but in this order: Queen, Four, Ace, Eight, King, Two, Seven, Five, Ten, Jack, Three, Six, Nine (so that, finally, the Queen is at the top of your face-down packet, the Nine at the bottom).

2 Spell the cards off, as described above, and the trick will work itself.

| TIPS |
| --- |
| • While picking up the Spades, it is a good idea to talk to the audience about the practical difficulties involved in teaching cards their names, or to indulge in some byplay with the audience – anything to disguise the fact that the order in which you are picking up the Spades is other than random. |
| • You can invent a mnemonic to help you remember the required order, but this can lead to confusion (two cards begin with "F," two with "S" and three with "T") so your best plan is probably just to learn the order – it doesn't take long. |

## TRICK 4

The magician asks a volunteer to shuffle the deck and deal out the cards into two equal packets; one for each of them. From his own packet he then selects a card and gives it to the magician, who puts it on top of her packet, followed by the rest of the volunteer's. The magician cuts the deck twice while asking the volunteer to name his card (e.g., the Three of Clubs). The magician then spells out the sentence Y-O-U-R C-A-R-D W-A-S T-H-E T-H-R-E-E O-F
C-L-U-B-S, turning up a card for each letter. The card turned up at the final "S" of the sentence is indeed the Three of Clubs.

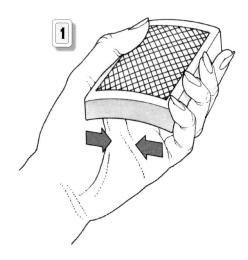

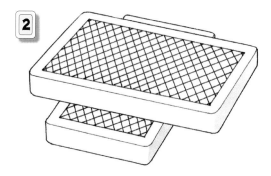

1 While the volunteer is choosing his card, squeeze the packet in your hand so that the 26 cards in it all gain a slight curve; this will be enough for you to keep this packet separate from the cards returned to you by the volunteer.

2 Once he has done so, it is easy enough to cut the deck first so that the chosen card goes to the bottom of the deck, and second so that the deck is returned to its original order, with the chosen card in the 26th position down from the top. The name of any card in the deck is spelled using between 10 and 15 letters, so all you have to do is choose the first part of the sentence according to the numerical value of the card's name. "Three of Clubs" has 12 letters, as do "Four of Hearts," "King of Spades," etc., so their names require a 14-letter prefix – e.g., "Your card was the." A 15-letter name (e.g. "Seven of Diamonds") needs an 11-letter prefix (e.g., "You chose the"), a 14-letter name (e.g., "Jack of Diamonds") a 12-letter prefix (e.g., "This card is the"), a 13-letter name (e.g., "Queen of Spades") a 13-letter prefix (e.g., "Your card is the"), an 11-letter name (e.g., "Ace of Hearts") a 15-letter prefix (e.g., "You picked out the"), and a 10-letter name (e.g., "Six of Clubs") a 16-letter prefix (e.g., "Here's your card, the").

To avoid calculating the number of letters in a card's name each time from scratch, memorize that "of Diamonds" has 10 letters, "of Hearts" and "of Spades" each have 8, and that "of Clubs" has 7.

### TIP

- While cutting the deck, seemingly at random, you may be able to glance at the chosen card and will not need to ask the volunteer what it was. This obviously adds to the magical effect.

# NOT IN THE CLUB

♣

From 14 cards, 13 of which are Clubs, pick out the intruder from a different suit with speed and ease while blindfolded!

The magician explains that the suit of Clubs derived its name not from weaponry, or from one of the suits of the Tarot pack (as the more educated may suspect), but from the fact that the cards of that suit are extremely clubbable types: like any old-fashioned gentlemen's club, they tend to be strict about the rules of admission, and to blackball "anyone of the wrong suit" who tries to join them.

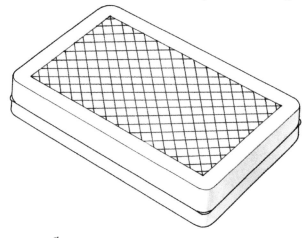

1 Before this trick, prepare the Clubs by very gently using fine sandpaper to round down the four corners of the packet. The amount removed should be very small.

2 To demonstrate the story you have told, select the 13 Clubs from a full deck and pass them as one packet and the remainder of the deck as another to a volunteer. Ask him to take any card from the rest of the deck and shuffle it into the packet of Clubs. Once he has done so, ask him to blindfold you (or call a second volunteer to do this while the first is manipulating the cards) and then to pass you the packet. Though the discrepancy between the cards will go unnoticed when the cards are in normal use, it will be easy enough to detect any single card in the packet whose corners have *not* been rounded. You will be able to pull out the intruding card – a feat you can perform again and again.

---

**TIPS**

- Once you have performed this basic trick a couple of times, vary things.
- Ask the volunteer sometimes to give you an unadulterated packet of Clubs, sometimes to put more than one "intruder" into the packet, without telling you which he is doing.

---

# CARDS THAT COUNT

These tricks rely on adding the values of cards together
to predict a volunteer's choice.

This is a self-working trick. At the outset, deal 10 cards, although there is no need to draw attention to this fact: either count *sotto voce* or count as far as 11 and stop just before you drop that card onto the heap. Either way, as you return the heap to the deck, catch a glimpse of its bottom card (e.g., the Ten of Hearts).

### TRICK 1

The magician counts out a number of cards from the top of the deck while remarking to the audience that the power of magic is present in everyone's mind, but that in most cases it is unrealized. Returning the dealt cards to the deck, she adds that, for example, everybody present has the subconscious knowledge of where in the deck every card is – for example, the Ten of Hearts. To prove this, she asks someone to give her a number between 10 and 20 and then with some counting and dealing comes up with the Ten of Hearts.

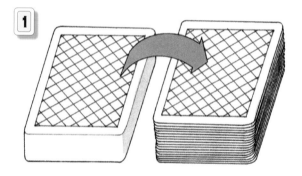

1 Ask a volunteer for a number (e.g., 17), and count the cards out as before, this time 17 of them. Putting the rest of the deck to one side, pick up the packet of 17 cards and add the digits of the number 17 together: $1 + 7 = 8$.

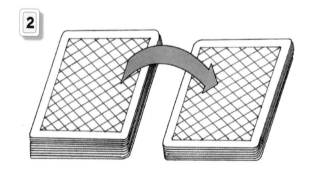

2 Deal eight cards from the top of the packet, and it will be the Ten of Hearts.

## TRICK 2

The magician gives a volunteer a set of nine cards, running from Ace to Nine in mixed suits, turns her back, and asks him to lay them out in three rows. He is then asked to select any one of the cards and remove it from the array. After asking the volunteer to make some calculations, still with her back turned, she tells him immediately the card he chose.

1 Ask the volunteer to lay the cards out and remove one, as described above. Then ask him to think of the cards in each row as digits making up a three-figure number – e.g., a row showing Four, Eight and Six would be regarded as 486 – and to add up the three rows, with the gap where he removed a card being counted as a 0. Once he has completed the addition, he must add up the digits of the total and give her the answer. Determining the numerical value of the chosen card is easy: you simply subtract the volunteer's final total from either 9 (if less than 9), 18 (if between 9 and 17) or 27 (if 18 or greater). A simple mathematical principle determines that the result of your subtraction is the correct numerical value.

2 The secret of identifying the card's suit is that, while the suits of the nine cards *seem* random, in fact they are not: you set them up beforehand. There are various mnemonics you can use to remember what they are. An easy one is to think of the order of precedence of the suits in games like bridge: Spades, Hearts, Diamonds, Clubs. The first two suits represent odd numbers, the second pair even numbers. As Spades are superior to Hearts, they represent more numbers: 1 (Ace), 5 and 9 are Spades, while the intervening odd numbers, 3 and 7, are Hearts. Following a similar line of reasoning, 2 and 6 are Diamonds and 4 and 8 are Clubs.

### TIPS

• This trick can be repeated three or four times, with your back still turned and with different volunteers laying out the cards in any ordering of three rows of three, and becomes more impressive with the repetition.
• Do not use too simple a mnemonic; for example, someone might notice if all the black cards were odd and all the red ones even.

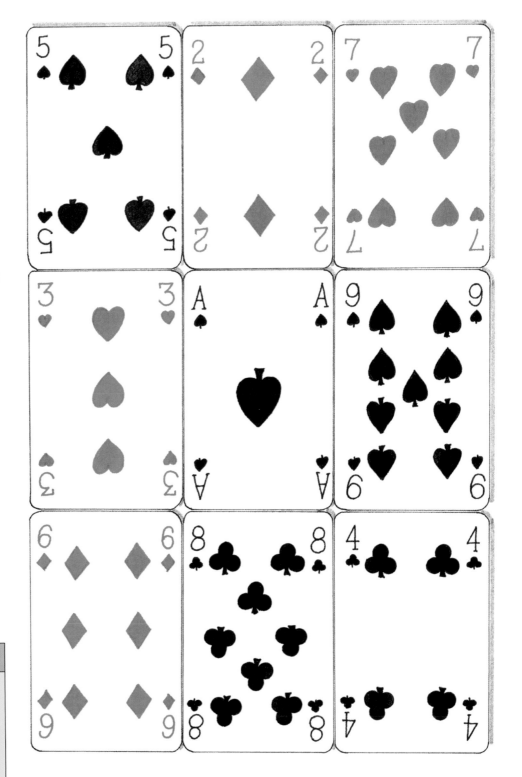

## TRICK 3

The magician deals off the top 10 cards from the deck, face-up, and asks a volunteer to count the numerical value of the cards (with Jack = 11, Queen = 12 and King = 13). While he is announcing the total to the rest of the audience, the magician returns the cards to the deck and repeats the process with the next 10 cards from the top. When these are added up they give a different total. This time, while the volunteer is adding up the figures and announcing the result, the magician is writing something on a sheet of paper, which she folds and passes to a different member of the audience. Taking back the second packet from the volunteer, she tells him that what she has written down is a prediction of the total of 10 cards that he himself will deal. She cuts the deck at random, hands him the lower packet, and he counts out 10 cards, and then adds up their value. His result is 70, and this proves to be the number the magician wrote down.

1 This trick requires a stacked deck. Separate the Twos, Sevens and Queens from the rest of the pack. Take one numerical set from the remainder, in mixed suits, and lay it out in a shuffled row; for example, Three, Five, Jack, King, Nine, Ace, Four, Six, Eight, Ten.

2 From the remaining 30 cards, choose another numerical set in mixed suits and lay it out in a row below the first one, following the same random order.

3 Do this two more times and then collect up the rows as four packets to make a deck of 40 cards.

4 Thoroughly shuffle the 12 cards you earlier discarded and put them at the top of the deck.

5 Once the first 10 cards have been counted, use the volunteer announcing the total to cover the fact that you are not returning all of the cards to the top of the deck – only about half of them, with the remainder going to the bottom. The second time, put the whole packet of 10 back on top of the deck. Thereafter the trick works itself.

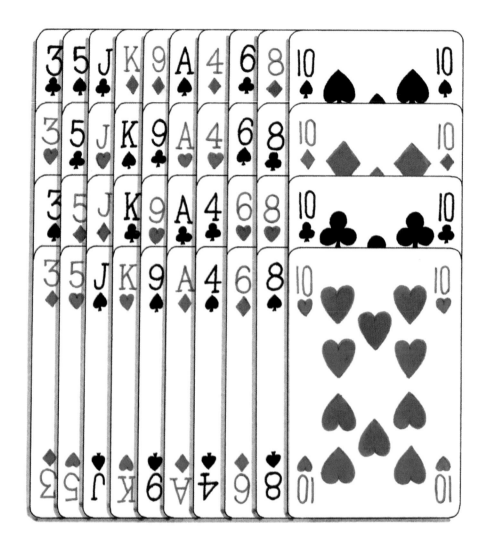

### TIPS

- Between different performances you can vary the total by excluding a different trio of numbers – for example, if you discarded the Twos, Eights and Queens rather than the Twos, Sevens and Queens, the total of the volunteer's cards would always be 69.
- You can add to the effect by allowing the volunteer to make the cut himself, relying on the fact that he will almost certainly cut the deck somewhere near the middle. If he does not, immediately grab the cards from him on some pretext (e.g., it's a new deck and the cards may be sticking together – no, everything seems all right), and then return the deck. It is extremely unlikely that he will be so perverse a second time.

# THE WHITE RABBIT'S CARD TRICK

♠

Introduce this trick by explaining that it was taught to Alice by the White Rabbit, but that Alice forgot about it when telling Lewis Carroll of her adventures.

This trick works itself, but can be performed only at certain times of the day – 12:16, 13:15, 1:27, 14:14, 15:13, 3:25, 16:12, 4:24, 17:11, 5:23, 18:10, 6:22, 19:09, 7:21, 20:08, 8:20, 21:07, 9:19, 22:06, 10:18, 23:05 and 11:17.

The beauty of this trick is that the option presented to the volunteers of choosing which packet to place the cards on seems to prevent any prior calculation by you of the position of the card, whereas in fact – as a little thought reveals – it makes no difference whatsoever to the position.

Ask four volunteers to choose cards, and then ask them to decide among themselves which one of those four they like the best. While they are discussing the matter, deal the rest of the deck into two equal packets.

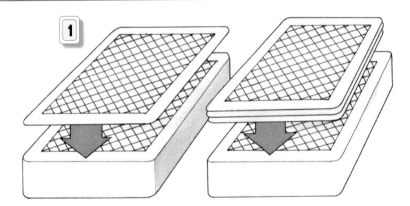

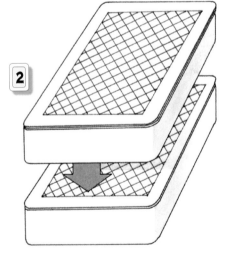

1 Receive back the cards, but don't look at them. Then ask the volunteers to select which packet they would like the chosen card to be placed on and which packet they'd like the other three cards to be placed on, and follow their requests.

2 Put one packet on top of the other, making sure that the packet with the chosen card is placed underneath. Glance at your watch (which is what the White Rabbit did when showing the trick to Alice) and announce the time – e.g., 5:23. Ask one of the volunteers to add these two numbers to give you the result – 28 – and obediently count down through the deck to reveal that the 28th card is indeed the chosen one.

# HOLEY HANDKERCHIEF

◆

In this trick, a card appears to drop through a thick handkerchief.

A volunteer picks a card, and then returns it to the deck. The magician produces a handkerchief, passes it around for examination and drapes it over the deck to demonstrate that it is completely opaque – there is no way that she or anyone else can tell what the cards are through it. She then takes the deck and wraps it in the handkerchief. Holding the package by its "tail," she gives it a few jerks, and suddenly a card drops through the cloth. It proves, of course, to be the chosen card. Handkerchief and deck can then be examined.

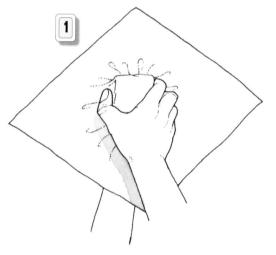

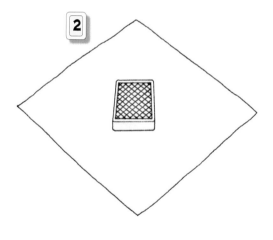

When the volunteer has picked a card, ask him to examine it, then return it to the deck. Execute the pass (see pages 14–15) to bring the chosen card to the top.

1 Drape the handkerchief (with one corner pointing towards you) over the face-down deck, but as you withdraw the deck with one hand, leave the other hand, still holding the chosen card, under the handkerchief (which really *is* opaque!).

2 Immediately place the deck face-down on top of the handkerchief, over the chosen card.

| TIP |
| --- |
| • You can borrow a handkerchief from the audience if you like, but that is always a bit of a gamble – especially if the audience are children! You need the handkerchief to be opaque, clean and large enough, so it is probably best to resist the temptation of gaining added effect by borrowing one. |

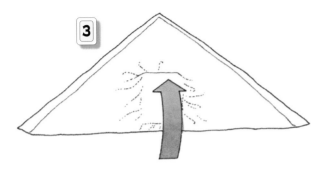

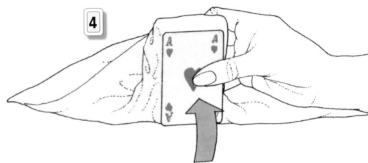

3 Flip the near corner of the cloth up and over the deck.

4 With your free hand, grip the deck (through the cloth) and the chosen card and turn the package vertically towards you, so that you can now see the chosen card.

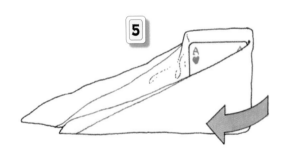

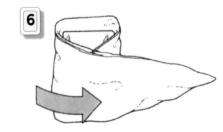

5 Take one of the loose-hanging flaps of handkerchief and fold it towards the other side.

6 Then take both flaps and fold them back again, tugging on the cloth so that the folds hold the chosen card tightly in place.

7 You can now dangle the package by its "tail" reasonably casually until you decide to start jerking it, at which time the chosen card will shake free.

# TOPSY-TURVY GAMBLE

## Identify a volunteer's secret card from a topsy-turvy, jumbled deck.

The magician announces that she has had one drink too many and, buoyed by Dutch courage, is going to bet a volunteer about the identity of a card selected at random from a jumbled deck. Stressing that she has only one chance in 52 of getting it right, she says that she is willing to bet a world cruise against his watch that she will win. When the volunteer looks dubious about the safety of his watch, she increases the difference: a world cruise with a star celebrity of his choice against any old scrap of paper he can find in his pocket.

The stakes settled, ask the volunteer to shuffle the cards, then take the deck back from him. The card on which you are betting is the top card of the deck before the start of the manipulation. The best way to determine which that is, is to glimpse the bottom card of the deck as the volunteer gives the cards back to you after shuffling, then swiftly use the pass (see pages 14–15) to take that card to the top.

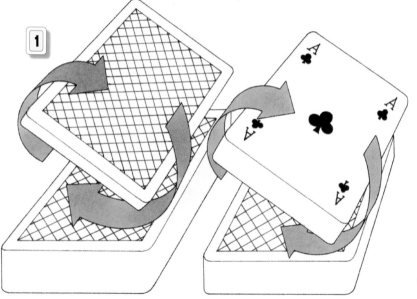

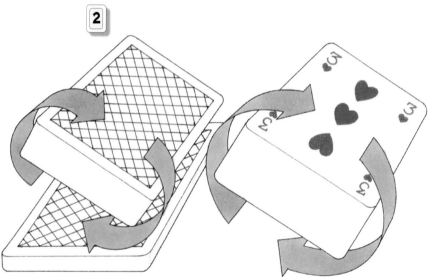

1 Saying that you will jumble not only the order of the cards but even the way they are facing, you then pull off a packet from the deck, turn it over and replace it face-up on the deck. Repeat this with another, larger, packet.

2 Repeat again with another, yet larger packet. Finally, turn the whole deck over so that everything will be completely muddled.

## TIPS

- Practice the manipulation until you can do it naturally, without having to pause and count how many times you have flipped packets over.
- Bearing in mind the size of the stakes involved, it is a **very good idea** to make sure you have not, in fact, had one drink too many before the performance!

3 Announce what your card is (e.g., the Two of Clubs), and it will be the first face-down card you come to as you fan through the deck.

# THE VAIN CARD

♥

## Make a chosen card appear from the middle of a deck.

### TRICK 1

The magician asks a volunteer to pick a card from the deck, show it to his companions, and then return it. While shuffling the deck, she explains to the audience that the cards can be as guilty of the minor sins as human beings are – and especially of the sin of vanity. In particular, the card that was selected has become overly proud of the fact that it was chosen from among the other 51 – indeed, there is nothing the magician can do to stop it from rising from the middle of the deck to accept the audience's applause.

> ### TIPS
>
> - You can enhance the effect by touching a fingertip of your right hand to the top of the card as it rises, giving the illusion that the fingertip is pulling, or is being pushed up by, the card.
> - Alternatively, if it's hot, you can press the deck hard against your forehead, as if concentrating, and then remove the rest of the deck to leave the rear card (i.e., the chosen one) stuck to your forehead.
> - This trick can be neatly linked with the next. Continue your patter along the lines of: "You think this is just a trick? You don't believe me? Well, look, I'll speak sternly to the cards, but it won't do any good." You should then force the same card onto another volunteer – it doesn't matter too much if your attempt is unsuccessful – and proceed.

**1** As soon as the card is returned to the deck, use either version of the pass (see pages 14–15) to bring it to the top. The shuffle is of course a fake. When you display the "shuffled" deck to the audience with the selected card at its rear, hold the deck between your thumb on one side and your third and little fingers on the other.

**2** This leaves your middle two fingers behind the deck, hidden from view, and you can use them simply to "walk" the card slowly upwards. To the audience, a little distance from you, it looks as if the card is emerging from somewhere in the center of the deck, an illusion you have reinforced with your patter.

## TRICK 2

In the customary way, the magician invites a
volunteer to select a card and examine it, and then
to return it to the deck. Cards, explains the magician
as she shuffles, are as vain as human beings, and she
knows for a fact that this particular card will now
consider itself superior to all its fellows. As proof,
she fans out the deck face-down, and sure enough
the selected card has turned itself the opposite way
from the rest, so that it shows face-up.

1 While the volunteer is looking at his card,
showing it to those around him, etc., turn over the
bottom card of the deck, so it is face-up against the
face of the next card (see the last straight shuffle
deception, page 11).

2 Proffer the deck to the volunteer for him to push
his card into it. The deck looks face-down when, in
fact, all the cards except the top one are face-up.

3 Turn the deceiving card back the way it was,
which you can do in the course of performing the
shuffle. Fan out the deck face-down to show the
selected card, face-up.

### TIPS

- This trick is best done in conjunction
  with the previous one.
- It is advisable not to repeat it,
  because someone is sure to figure
  out what's happening if you do it
  too many times.

# THE SCURVY KNAVES

Simple techniques can make cards appear to move
position in a deck, all by themselves!

### TRICK 1

Once upon a time, the magician tells her audience, there were not one but four scurvy knaves who stole the Queen of Hearts' tarts. She pulls out the four criminals – i.e., the four Jacks – from the deck to show them to the audience, and then places them on top of the deck. The Royal Guards, she explains, chased the knaves until finally they were trapped in a single tower, where they hid. The first of them hid on the first floor (she puts one Jack at the bottom of the deck), the next hid on the second floor (she puts a Jack in the lower part of the deck), the third near the top of the tower (a Jack in the upper part of the

deck), and the fourth was so terrified he shinned right up the flagpole (the final Jack remains at the deck's top). When the Guards came charging in at the base of the tower the thief at the top was so frightened he jumped from his perch (she removes him from the top of the deck and shows him to the audience), and the others all moved up one place. As the Guards came up through the tower, each of the thieves in turn in desperation climbed the flagpole and jumped off (she peels off the remaining Jacks one by one).

> ### TIP
>
> • The technique of using three, already palmed, cards is so well known that it is advisable either to use the pass (see pages 14–15) or, by contrast, to use the palming technique (see pages 12–13) and then, as the trick ends, to grin, say something like, "Of course, every schoolchild knows *that* trick – but the story really did happen, and it happened like *this*," and then proceed to perform the next trick.

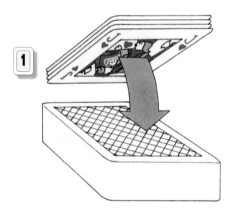

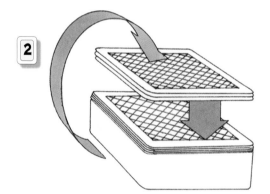

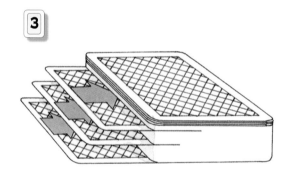

1 The trick begins with your placing the Jacks on top of the deck.

2 Swiftly use the pass (see pages 14–15) three times to bring three random cards from the bottom to cover them. Alternatively, when you are showing the four Jacks to the audience, already have three palmed cards behind them. Either way, the trick then works itself.

3 Continue telling the story, as described, pushing the three random cards into the deck and peeling the Jacks off from the top of the deck.

## TRICK 2

The magician tells the tale of the Queen of Hearts' tarts, and of how the Royal Guards chased the thieves until they were cornered in one of the Palace towers (see Trick 1). She explains how one of the criminals fled all the way up the flagpole at the top of the tower, and the second thief stayed on the first floor, and puts a Jack at the top and bottom of the deck.

Putting down the deck on the table in front of her and cutting it, the magician tells how the remaining two Jacks – both red or both black – were brothers, as can be seen by their colors. They stuck together and, worried equally by the prospects of Royal Paratroopers from above and Royal Tunnelers from below, ended up rather indecisively clutching each other for comfort halfway up the tower: she places them in the middle of the deck.

In fact the brothers were right to worry: the various divisions of Guards drove one thief down from the flagpole and another up from the first floor, so that all four were in the middle of the tower when finally arrested – as the magician demonstrates by splaying out the deck to show all four Jacks at its center.

### TIPS

- As noted, your patter is extremely important if the audience are to be distracted from the very simple cheat you are performing.
- You might like to plant an accomplice in the audience to further distract attention: she can be a rowdy, difficult customer, constantly yelling that she knows this trick and accusing you of performing the preceding trick – i.e., The Scurvy Knaves (1). Her gibes and your demonstrations of innocence (no palmed cards, etc.) should create enough diversion for the real mechanism to go unnoticed.

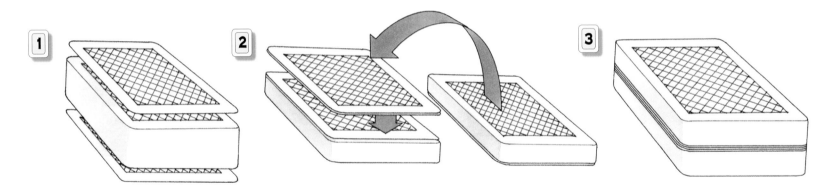

1 The Jacks will have been separated out from the deck during Trick 1. As you begin the story, show the Jacks clearly to your audience. Place the first Jack on top of the deck and the second underneath.

2 At the second stage of the story, the cut is the phony, and it is important that your patter be so involved and entertaining that no one thinks too much about it. When you cut the cards, make sure you know which packet is which. You put the two "brothers" into the center of the deck by placing them on top of what was the *upper* packet, and then place the other packet on top of that.

3 This brings together the four Jacks in the middle of the deck. Splay the deck to show them.

# Mutus Nomen Cocis Dedit

This trick depends on remembering a piece of dog Latin –
*Mutus Nomen Cocis Dedit* – to identify a pair of cards chosen secretly by a volunteer.

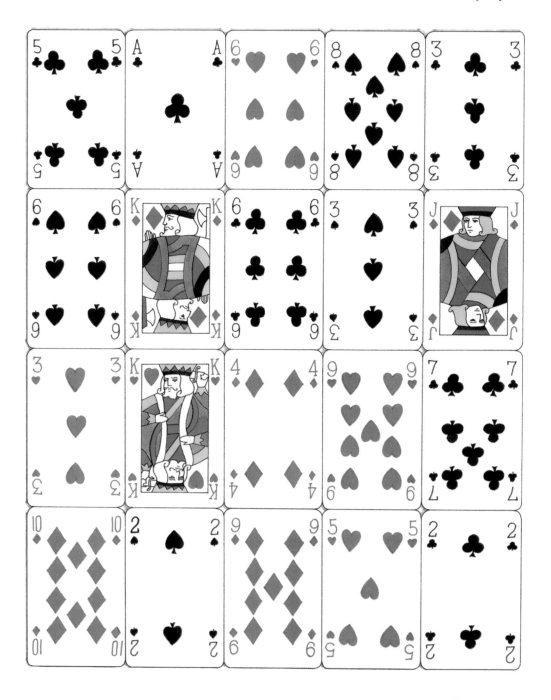

The magician asks a volunteer to shuffle the deck and then to deal the top 20 cards from it in the form of 10 pairs; the remainder of the deck is put to one side. He must then decide on one of the pairs, but not tell the magician which that is. She then gathers together the 20 cards and sets them out on the table in random order in four rows of five, and asks the volunteer to locate the now separated cards of his pair, but again not to tell her which they are; instead, all she asks is that he divulge the row or rows in which the two cards appear. As soon as he does so, she is able to identify the cards.

1 When you are laying out the 20 cards, the order in which you do so is not random at all. Instead you imagine that the letters of four Latin words are laid out in front of you (see illustration, left):

Place the first card at the top left corner of this imaginary grid, in the position denoted "M"; the second card goes at the center of the second row, in the other position denoted "M." The next two cards go in the two positions denoted "U," and so on until the grid is complete.

2 The information as to the row or rows in which the two cards appear is, as you can see, sufficient for you to identify the volunteer's pair.

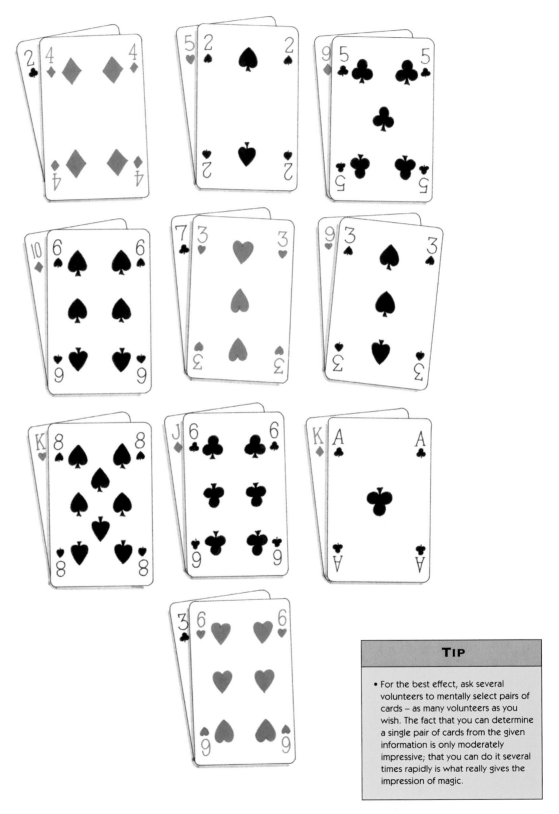

# RECITING THE DECK

Amaze the audience with your extraordinary powers, as you predict the identity of cards arranged in what seems to be a completely random sequence.

### TRICK 1

The magician passes out a deck of cards so that a volunteer from the audience can shuffle it. As it is being passed back to her, she notices that another member of the audience looks dissatisfied, so she insists that he shuffle it as well. Still muttering about skeptics and directing angry glares and insults at him, she returns the deck to her table, and proceeds to turn up the cards one by one, calling out each one before she turns it up. To general amazement – not least that of the skeptical audience member, whom she is still insulting – she is right every time.

## TIPS

- It is very unlikely that the audience will notice the regularity of the ordering.
- However, if you are worried about it, run the order of suits backwards and forwards: Clubs, Diamonds, Hearts, Spades, Spades, Hearts, Diamonds, Clubs, Clubs . . . Or you can vary things by having two Clubs in a row followed by a Diamond, a Heart and a Spade; then a Club, two Diamonds, a Heart and a Spade: then a Club, a Diamond, two Hearts and a Spade; and so on.

1 Prepare a deck ordered as follows: Ace of Clubs, Eight of Diamonds, Five of Hearts, Four of Spades, Jack of Clubs . . . This order seems random to the audience, but in fact it is not. What you have done is set the cards in two alphabetical orders at once: Clubs, Diamonds, Hearts, Spades and Ace, Eight, Five, Four, Jack, King, Nine, Queen, Seven, Six, Ten, Three, Two.

2 The "skeptic" can be any member of the audience: there is bound to be someone whom you can at least pretend to see looking dubious. Divert attention to him while you swap the shuffled deck for the prepared one. Call out the cards as ordered in the prepared deck.

## TRICK 2

As in the previous trick, the magician passes out the deck to the audience for thorough shuffling. It can be returned directly to her or, as before, there can be a diversion as she accuses a member of the audience of excessive skepticism – if he demurs, she tells him that she has X-ray eyes and can see the thoughts bubbling through his brain, whatever the expression on his face might be saying. Once she has the deck again, she puts it behind her back for a final shuffle, and then casually shows both sides of it to the audience as she holds it up in front of her. Again (or for the first time) talking about her X-ray eyes, she proceeds to call out the name of each card correctly before pulling it from the back of the deck and throwing it (see page 16) to the audience for verification.

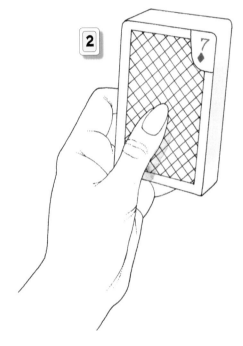

1 Once the deck has been shuffled by the audience and it is behind your back, do not, in fact, shuffle it. That is a lie to account for the movements of your arms as you do two things. Reverse the card at the top of the deck so that it is not face down but face up, and draw from a pocket or other place of concealment a card (perhaps the Joker) of the same or an identical deck, from which you have torn off the top left-hand corner and which you place face-down on the bottom of the deck. Bring the deck back into the view of the audience, making sure you have your thumb over the torn-away corner.

2 Hold the dummy face-up card towards the audience. You can now see the top corner of each card facing you and can read its value. Make a point of throwing each card to the audience for checking: in that way the spectators' attention will be drawn away from the fact that the cards are facing the wrong way as you pull them from the deck.

# CONFORMIST JACK

♥

When Conformist Jack is pushed into a deck of cards facing the wrong way, he magically turns over as he emerges from the other side.

The magician picks the Jack of Spades from the deck and tells the audience that this is well known by all students of cards to be the most conformist of any of the 52. "You wouldn't think so just to look at it," she remarks, passing it to the front row so that they can indeed look at it. Taking the card back, and with the deck held back-out towards the audience, its long edges upwards, she pushes the Jack, face-out, down through the deck until its bottom part protrudes below. Turning the deck over, though still keeping it back-out to the audience, she pushes the Jack back through it, but this time it emerges back-out like the other cards, having "conformed." Again the Jack can be inspected by the audience.

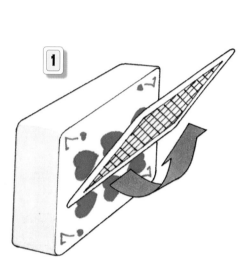

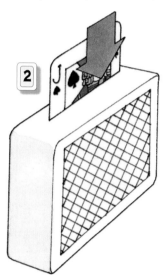

1 Cut the Jack of Spades from another deck in half horizontally, and have one of the halves palmed (see pages 12–13) face down in (say) your left hand. While the whole Jack is being inspected, palm the face-down top card of the deck in your right hand, and turn the deck over and place the palmed card face-down on the deck, which is otherwise face-up in your left hand with the half-card at its rear. Holding the deck face-out in your left hand, you can keep the half-card at the rear of the deck with the left hand's first finger.

2 Push the Jack downwards through the deck; it will look as if it is the only face-out card in the back-out deck. The half-card at the rear of the deck will now look like this.

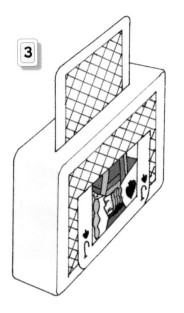

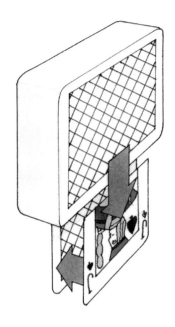

3 As you push the Jack through, tug it an extra little bit with the right hand. While giving the extra tug, use the right thumb to transfer the half-card to the rear of the protruding Jack. Start pushing the Jack upwards, simultaneously pushing the half-card a little into the deck.

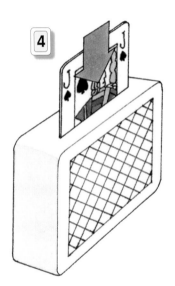

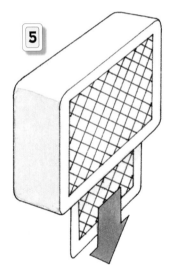

---

**TIP**

- As you give the Jack out, absent-mindedly splay the cards in your left hand a little, face-out, so that the observant will notice that the Jack did indeed emerge facing the same way as the others.

---

4 When turning the deck over, it is easy enough to turn it around at the same time – just perform the action flamboyantly, and the extra move will go unnoticed. The audience will think they are still seeing the face of the Jack, but in fact it is that of the half-card, with part of the Jack behind it.

5 Start pushing downwards again, and the real Jack will emerge, having apparently reversed itself while going through the deck. Give the Jack out for examination and put the deck "carelessly" on your table, spilling it a little. If anyone calls to inspect the deck, pick it up equally "carelessly," losing the half-card and "fumblingly" turning over the reversed card.

# JOKER'S DELIGHT

♠

**This trick begins with a Joker and two ordinary cards, but ends with three ordinary cards: the Joker seems to have disappeared!**

With a volunteer by her side, the magician holds up three cards – two nondescript cards with a Joker between them. She announces that the volunteer is going to play Find the Joker – just like Find the Lady – with the audience. Asking them to watch the cards carefully, she turns them face-down and very deliberately sets them out on the table in front of her. She tells the volunteer to move the cards around, but of course to keep his own eyes on the Joker so that he will know what he is doing. She lets him accept a couple of unsuccessful calls from the audience, and then asks him to turn up the Joker himself. It proves that the Joker has disappeared entirely, leaving a nondescript card in its place.

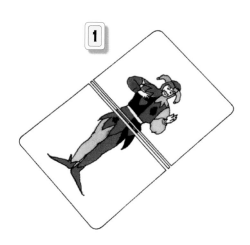

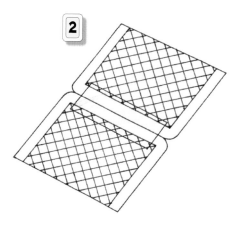

1 Beforehand, cut out a thin, central section from a Joker and throw it away, leaving yourself with the card's top and bottom.

2 Using clear tape, fix the edge of the top part of the Joker to the back of the edge of the lower part; turn it around so that the adhesive tape is on the inside of the fold.

3 Hang the assemblage over the top of another card, with part of the Joker showing to the front over the card's own face.

### TIP

• You might prefer to use a Queen rather than a Joker, so that this becomes really a case of Find the Lady. The point of using a Joker is so that you do not waste an entire deck.

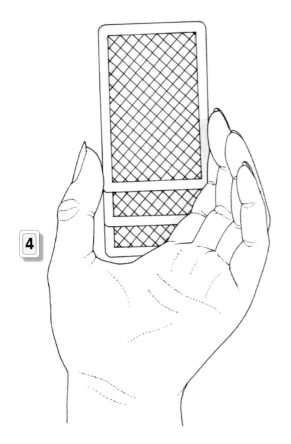

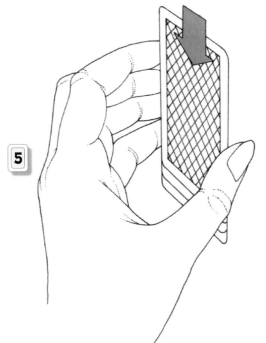

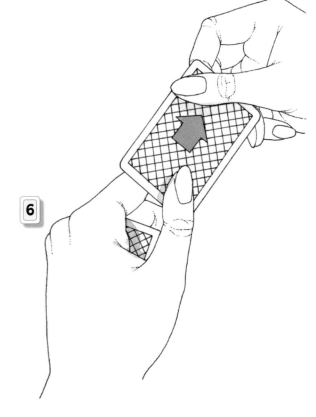

4 When you present the three cards they are one above the other, gripped at the sides, with the dummy card in the middle so that it looks like a Joker. Your grip is backhand, i.e., using the left hand, your thumb is on the left of the packet.

5 To deal out the cards, bring the hand down so that its back is upwards in front of you. Tap the card edges quickly on your table to shove what was the uppermost card through your hand and level with the rest.

6 Then (with the hand again back-upwards) pull the cards one by one from your hand to lay them on the table, leaving the assemblage in your hand. Get rid of it as soon as possible while the volunteer is distracting the audience by moving the cards around.

# SWAP

Cards can appear to swap places, with sleight of hand –
or a little help from some glue!

### TRICK 1

The magician shuffles the deck thoroughly and then gives half of it to a volunteer. She asks him to spread the cards of his packet out on the table and to draw a single card from the middle somewhere; she will do the same with her own half. She announces her chosen card (e.g., the Jack of Clubs) and asks him to tell his (e.g., the Seven of Spades). Both then put their cards on top of their own packets, gather the packets and cut them, so that the two cards are in the centers of their respective packets. The magician then proposes that they fan out their packets for a final look at the cards they drew. The volunteer discovers that the Jack of Clubs has migrated to his packet, and is not nestling right beside his own Seven of Spades.

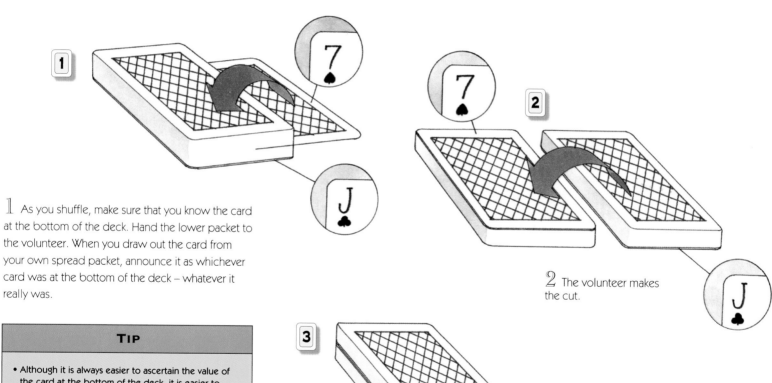

1 As you shuffle, make sure that you know the card at the bottom of the deck. Hand the lower packet to the volunteer. When you draw out the card from your own spread packet, announce it as whichever card was at the bottom of the deck – whatever it really was.

2 The volunteer makes the cut.

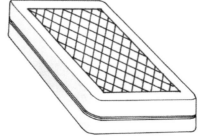

3 In doing so, he places his own card next to the Jack.

---

### TIP

- Although it is always easier to ascertain the value of the card at the bottom of the deck, it is easier to retain the top card in its position while performing the shuffle; moreover, there is a possibility that the volunteer may inadvertently notice the bottom card of the packet you hand him. Better, therefore, that the Jack of Clubs be at the top of the deck. If you like, you can give the cards a genuine shuffle, glimpse the bottom card, and then make the pass (see pages 14–15) to take it to the top.

### TRICK 2

The magician asks a volunteer to select two cards (e.g., the Three of Spades and the King of Hearts) and show them to the audience. She gives him an end-opening box (a card-box is fine) and asks him to put both cards into it. She tells the company that she knows what intelligent and observant people they are, and how nervous she is performing in front of such a discerning crowd – they won't have any trouble keeping track of just two cards, will they?

So saying, she takes back the box, pulls one card (e.g., the King of Hearts) out of it, and places that card face-down on the table. Obviously the card left in the box will be the Three of Spades; there's no need, she blusters, to check. The audience makes sounds of discontent, so she tells the volunteer to take a look: sure enough, the Three is still in the box. Picking up the King of Hearts and showing it, she returns it to the box, and this time pulls out the Three of Spades, which she displays ostentatiously as she returns to the table. Again, the volunteer checks the contents of the box. He finds the Three of Spades there, and, looking surprised, the magician turns up the card on the table to show it has become the King of Hearts.

1 The gimmick for this trick is a double-sided card, which you can make by carefully pasting back-to-back the Three of Spades and King of Hearts from an old deck, using a warm iron to make the face as thin as possible. (You can buy printed double-sided cards, but they rarely look convincing.) Place the dummy card on your table before the trick begins, with the King face-down. The eyeline of your audience must be on or below the level of your table, so that they cannot see the face-down card from above. Force the two cards on the volunteer using the Riffle Force or Cut it Yourself (see pages 16–17).

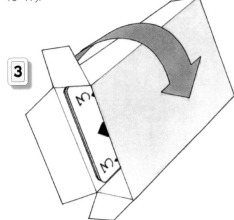

2 When you take out the King, place it face-down on the table. Let the volunteer check the contents of the box. When you pick up the King to "return" it to the box, pick up the dummy instead. Take the box from the volunteer, pull out the Three of Spades, put it on top of the "King," and return both cards to the box.

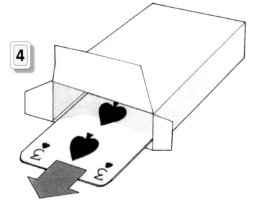

3 Start to give the box back to the volunteer but change your mind halfway. This action will allow you to turn the box over.

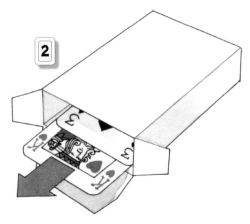

4 When you open the box for a second time, the Three of Spades side of the dummy card will be uppermost. Pull out the dummy, displaying the Three of Spades side as you return to your table. Place the dummy card on the table next to the real King. At the final revelation, simply pick up the real King of Hearts, so that both cards and the box can safely be examined by the audience.

<table>
<tr><td>

**TIPS**

• When picking up the dummy from your table you are also, so far as the audience is concerned, turning up a card that you laid there face-down.
• To turn up the correct face of the dummy, take it by the edge closer to the audience and lift – otherwise you risk giving a glimpse of the wrong side.

</td></tr>
</table>

# HOPSCOTCH FROM THE DECK

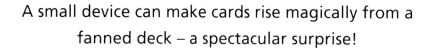

A small device can make cards rise magically from a
fanned deck – a spectacular surprise!

The magician goes among the audience and offers
the fanned deck to three volunteers, asking each to
select a card. As they examine these, she returns to
the front of the audience, shuffling. As the cards are
passed back to her, she inserts each into the deck
and then goes towards her table. Holding up the
deck in a fan, face-out to the audience, she asks the
volunteers to concentrate on the cards they chose.
Slowly, one by one, these rise from the fan, and she
passes them back to the volunteers as keepsakes.

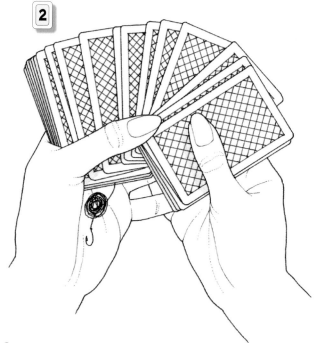

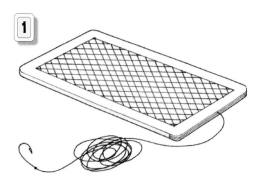

1 This trick involves a quite elaborate gimmick
which is a box, its length and breadth just greater
than those of a card and the thickness of six or seven
cards; it has a card-face stuck to one side of it and a
card-back to the other, and its interior is divided into
three partitions – old cards can be used to make the
dividers, while the box itself can be constructed of
thin card or tin.

To the inside of the top center of the box is
attached a black thread, at the other end is a
sharp hook.

2 When offering the fanned cards, keep the box at
the bottom of the deck, shielded by a few bunched
cards; have its open end towards you, and keep the
deck fairly close to your body, with the thread
coiled in your hand. The purpose of the casual
shuffle you give the deck as the volunteers are
examining their cards is both to bring the box to the
center of the deck and to turn the deck around, so
that the opening now faces the audience with the
thread running up over the box's aperture and the
top of the deck.

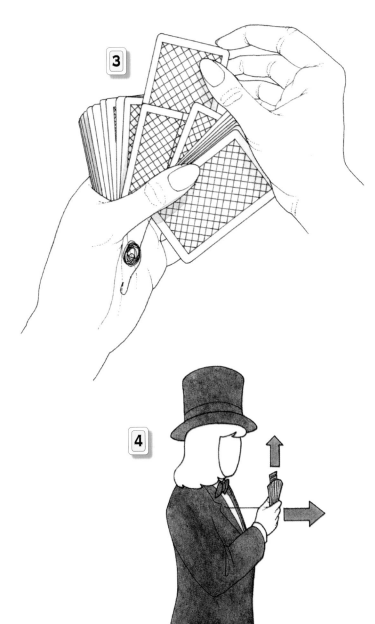

3 Push the returned cards into the box in inverse order, if you can, with the first above the second above the third. Each card pushes down a section of black thread.

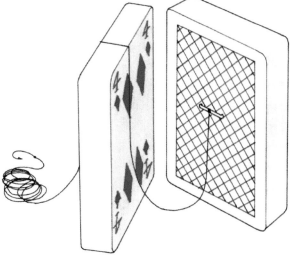

For a less elaborate gimmick using the same principle, staple the end of a thread to the center of a card, which you retain near the bottom of the deck. Proceed much as above, pushing the returned cards into the deck against the thread looped over the ends of the other cards.

4 As you return to your table, with your back to the audience, attach the hook to the front of your costume. Do not fan the deck too broadly as you hold it up to the audience. Slowly extend your arm, and the first card will climb up from the rest. As soon as it is about one-third of the way out, pluck it from position, gather and re-fan the cards, and extend your arm again to repeat the process to reveal the other two cards.

---

**TIPS**

- The advantage of the box is that you make the chosen cards rise from a fanned deck; with the simpler gimmick the deck must be held gathered.
- The purpose of giving the chosen cards away as souvenirs is to offer you a pretext for putting the deck to one side, so that you can use a new deck for your next trick.

# TWISTING CARD

In a deck of cards with a ribbon threaded through it, a chosen card reveals itself by twisting around to face the other way.

The magician produces a deck of cards through one end of which a hole has been punched. She asks a volunteer to choose a card and return it to the deck. Shuffling, she goes to her table and picks up a length of ribbon, which she passes to the volunteer for checking. She then threads the ribbon through the hole and asks him to tie the loose ends tightly. She fans out the cards for one last check, blindfolds him (or has a second volunteer do that for her), and then puts the knot in his hand, letting the deck hang beneath. She says: "You know what your card is but can't see it; it's about time you let the rest of us see it, even though we don't know what it is." She asks him to give the ribbon a jerk, and one card is discovered to have reversed itself in the deck. On removal of his blindfold, the volunteer confirms that this is indeed his card.

You can use any of the forcing techniques (pages 16–17) to make sure his selection is a particular card (eg, the Six of Spades).

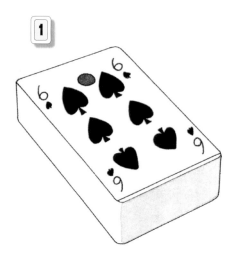

1 This particular Six of Spades has been drawn from an identical deck and has its end (the opposite end from the hole) shaved off to distinguish it from the other cards in the deck.

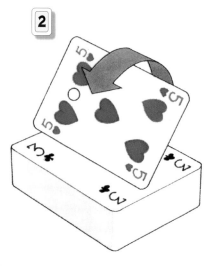

2 While he is examining it, palm (see pages 12–13) the top card of the deck and surreptitiously turn the deck over, returning the palmed card face-down to the top of the now face-up deck.

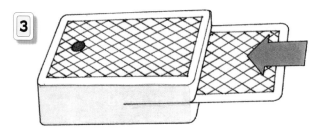

3 Offer it to him for him to push his card back in. You can splay the deck a little, for this. When you return to your table, again palm off the reversed top card and unobtrusively dump it or reverse it.

### TIPS

- This trick operates much better with ribbon (as described) than with string.
- White ribbon makes the extra loop around the end of the Six much less noticeable than would any other color.

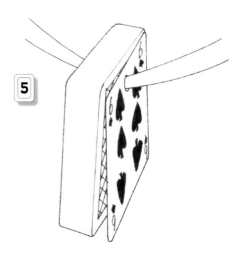

4 Cut the deck casually at the point indicated by the short card, as if it were easier to maneuver the ribbon through two halves rather than the whole deck at once.

5 Carefully thread the lower half, including the face-up Six.

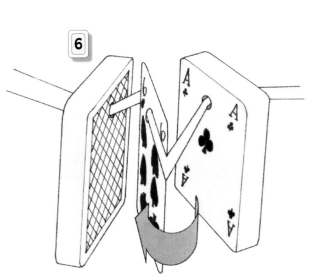

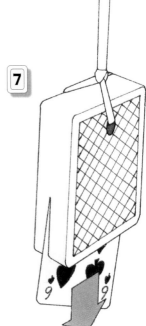

6 Then thread the upper half, but have some slight difficulty just as you are finishing, so that with your non-ribbon hand you can rotate the doctored Six, turning it face-down like all the others. Grip the deck tightly while the volunteer ties the knot, and tug against him to tighten the loop of ribbon around the turned card. He is the only person who might notice the loop, which is why you have him blindfolded.

7 When the volunteer jerks the ribbon, his chosen card appears.

# MAGIC TRICKS

PETER ELDIN

# INTRODUCTION

Generally, all books on magic explain the secret methods whereby the tricks are accomplished. This book is no exception. But let me tell you the greatest secret of magic – a secret that often takes magicians many years to discover, and which many never discover at all. That great secret is that the secret of a trick is the least important part of the trick!

In magic it matters little what you do. What matters most is how you do it. "It's not what you do but the way that you do

it" is an adage that is particularly appropriate to conjuring.

One of the tricks in this book is The Rising Cards, a trick that has baffled and entertained audiences all over the world. Many years ago a book was published describing some two hundred different methods of accomplishing this trick! Since that book was published, magicians have devised many more methods. The methods may vary but the essentials of the trick remain the same – selected cards rise from the pack of their own accord. So, no matter what method is used, the trick remains essentially the same. And that is why the so-called secrets of magic are not the most important part.

When reading the instructions for a trick, do not dismiss the method as being too simple. Some of the simplest of tricks are the most deceptive. Practice each trick and when you are sure that you can do it well, show it to a friend. You may be as amazed as your friend – amazed that such a simple method can fool someone.

Do not try to learn all the tricks at once. By all means read through the whole of this book to get a general idea of what magic is all about. Then pick just one or two tricks and learn them thoroughly. Only when you are confident that you can do these tricks well should you go on to learn another trick. It has been said that "Slow but sure wins the race," slow but sure is certainly the way to achieve success in performing magic.

None of the instructions given in this book is sacrosanct. If you are at all uncomfortable about a particular aspect of a trick, see if you can change it to suit your own style. An obvious example is where you are told to take something in a particular hand. If you are happier

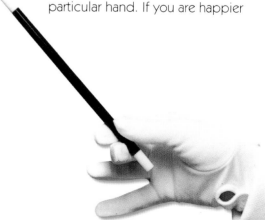

using the other hand, then do so. No two magicians do the same trick in the same way – well, not if they have given any thought to their magic. One of the most interesting aspects of magic is that its performance is changing constantly.

At first you may go through the motions of a performance like a robot. But gradually, as you gain confidence and experience, the real you will come to the fore and your performances will be enhanced as a result.

It has been said that a good magician is really an actor playing the part of a magician. This means that you have got to believe in your magical abilities and to play the part of a magician. At first you may find this difficult to do because you are concentrating on the mechanics of the trick. That is why so many books on magic urge you to practice as much as possible. The emphasis is on the mechanics because the mechanics are unimportant. That may sound weird but the reason is that you must practice thoroughly, so the mechanics become automatic.

When you can do a trick without thinking, you can then concentrate on presenting your magic in a professional manner. It is somewhat similar to driving a car; at first the new driver is thinking, "Should I change gear or am I going at the wrong speed?" An experienced driver does not think, "Should I change gear?" He just does it. A better analogy might be with a tennis player who does not consciously think, "I must reach out to hit that ball and put some top spin on it to fool my opponent."

He just does it. It takes practice; and experience; it may even take a few knocks; but keep at it and you will get there in the end.

Many of the actual mechanics used by magicians are incredibly simple. It is even possible to buy tricks that are advertised as "self-working." The magician does not have to do anything – the trick does itself! Therein lies a danger. Tricks are often sold to tyro magicians with the assurance that there is "no skill required," or that the "trick is self-working." Don't believe it. There is no such thing as a self-working trick. If you want your magic to be successful, you have got to put work into it – even with "self-working" tricks. If you don't, you will just be someone performing tricks – a trained chimpanzee could do them just as well. But work at it, practice, make it

entertaining and a magical transformation takes place. No longer are you someone who just knows how to do a few tricks – you are a magician! Hard work always pays off in the end. The most important thing to remember is to imbue the trick with your own personality. You must be yourself, and you must perform in a way that is natural to you. This is not easy and it may take you some time before you can do it.

Please do not be a magic bore. You may like magic but the person you are boring may not. It is so easy to be a magic bore by showing trick after trick after trick. Keep to the old show-business saying, "Leave 'em wanting more." Just do one or two tricks at a time and people will come back. Do magic all night long and you could lose a lot of friends.

In this introduction you have been given quite a few dos and don'ts. Here comes the most important rule of them all: enjoy your magic. Don't take it too seriously. Have fun; that is what magic is all about.

# MAGIC THROUGH THE AGES

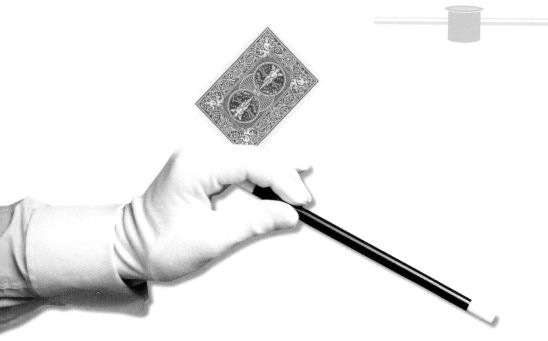

No-one knows for certain how old the art of magic is. It is probably as old as mankind itself. The first actual record of a magical performance for entertainment purposes dates from the times of the Ancient Egyptians – but conjuring was a well-established art long before that.

In the early days there was very little difference between conjuring and witch-craft – indeed the terms get mixed up even today. The original performers called upon their knowledge of all the sciences and it is from the days of these witch-doctors/magicians/priests that most of the modern sciences originated. Somewhere along the way the magical entertainer left the mumbo jumbo of witchcraft and the intellectual pursuit of science behind and began to ply his craft solely for the entertainment of others.

Even so these early performers were often accused of dark practices. The first book on conjuring in the English language was actually called *Discoverie of Witchcraft* but it explains many of the tricks that magicians still use to this day. One such trick is the Cups and Balls, in which balls appear and disappear beneath three cups. It is performed today using the same basic method described in *Discoverie of Witchcraft*. Its origins can be traced back to Ancient Rome, and it was probably known even earlier.

In the sixteenth century, when this book was published, the magicians were usually itinerant performers, doing their acts at local fairs and markets. Then things began to change and performers were more often to be seen in theaters. Most magicians of this time wore long, flowing robes and their tables were draped to the ground. In the mid-nineteenth century a French performer called Robert-Houdin did away with all this suspicious drapery and performed in regular evening dress with very little paraphernalia on stage. Originally a watchmaker, he brought a new inventive-ness to magic. He built many automata which were used in his shows and he was one of the first people to do a two-person mind-reading act. His magic was so good the French government even employed him to prevent a revolution!

Robert-Houdin is regarded as "the father of modern conjuring" and it is from his name that young Ehrich Weiss took his stage name, a name that lives to this day – Houdini, the greatest escape artist ever. His first big success came when he escaped from handcuffs in Scotland Yard, the headquarters of the British police. From that time on he was constantly in the public eye, making incredible escapes from straitjackets, boxes, jails, handcuffs, chains, and anything else that people invented to try and confine him.

Contemporaries of Houdini included some of the greatest names in magic – Harry Kellar, who ran away from home to become America's best known illusionist; T. Nelson Downs, who produced showers of coins from the air; Harry Blackstone, who was a master showman and whose son is today one of America's best known magicians; and Chung Ling Soo, the renowned Chinese magician. Chung Ling Soo's greatest trick was not revealed until after his death. Everyone thought he was Chinese, he even used an interpreter, but after his death his great secret was revealed – he was really an American named William Robinson.

When Houdini first visited Britain, the top British magician was John Nevil Maskelyne. In addition to being a superb magician, Maskelyne was a genius at making mechanical figures. Possibly the most famous of these was called Psycho. This figure of an Oriental could play cards so well that it could beat any member of the audience offering the challenge. As the figure was seated on a plinth of clear glass, there seemed no logical explanation as to how the figure was operated. Maskelyne did not confine his mechanical genius to magic; he also invented a lock for public toilets, a typewriter and a machine for issuing bus tickets, among others!

Maskelyne teamed up with another British magician, David Devant and together they dominated the British magical scene for many years. People who saw Devant called him the greatest British magician of all time. That accolade has now passed down to Paul Daniels who has done more to popularize magic in Britain than any other person. For over 15 years he has had a regular magic series on television. His shows have also brought some of the best magicians from around the world to the attention of British audiences.

In recent years many incredible magical spectaculars have been produced, particularly in America with superb magicians such as Siegfried and Roy, David Copperfield, Harry Blackstone, Jr., and Lance Burton. These colorful extravaganzas use all the modern theatrical effects available and cost many millions of dollars to produce. In spite of all this hi-tec wizardry to excite the public, there is still room for the more intimate performance in small theaters, restaurants or informal gatherings. Magic can be performed for just one person or for many persons, but it is equally effective in any situation provided that the performer has taken the time to learn the art of entertaining people.

# COIN IN BALL OF YARN

The magician borrows a coin and makes it disappear. It is later recovered in the center of a ball of yarn.

**You will need**
◊ a ball of yarn
◊ a special "slide" (This is simply a flattened tin tube but it must be wide enough to take any coin you are likely to be offered.)
◊ a coin
◊ a glass tumbler

1 Wind the yarn around the bottom portion of the slide. Now place the ball of yarn in a left-side coat pocket or behind some piece of equipment on your table. It must be in a position that you can "load" the coin into the slide with your left hand and then pull the slide from the yarn without your actions being obvious.

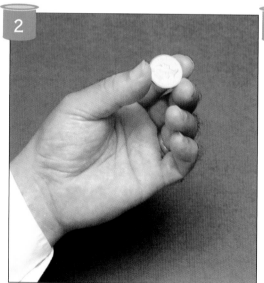

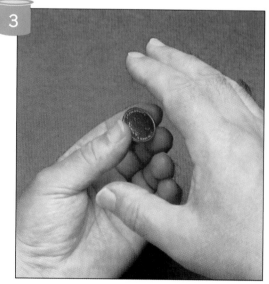

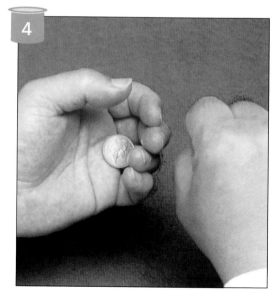

2 Borrow a coin from someone in your audience. Hold the coin between the tips of the thumb and forefinger of your left hand.

3 Bring your right hand over the coin as if to take it from the left. As soon as your right hand covers the coin, let the coin drop from your fingertips into the palm of your left hand.

4 As the coin drops, close your right hand as if taking the coin and move it away to the right. Look at your right hand as you do this and let your left hand fall away naturally.

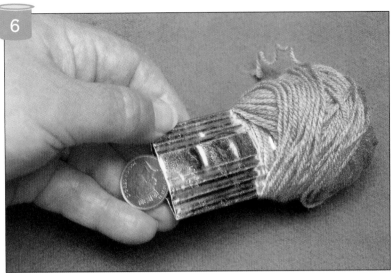

5 Make some comment about the fact that money does not last very long. Then, with a squeezing motion, open the fingers of your right hand. The coin has vanished! Try to forget that the coin is still hidden in your left hand. You must convince yourself that the coin has really vanished. If you do not convince yourself, you will not convince your audience.

**TIP**

• To prove that the coin revealed in the yarn is the very same coin that vanished, it is a good idea to have a small gummed sticker available. The spectator can stick this to the coin and sign it if so wished to prove that no substitution takes place. With an unusual coin, such as one of foreign currency, this will not be necessary.

6 While still gazing at your right hand in amazement, reach over with your left hand to recover the ball of yarn. Let the secreted coin enter the slide and then pull the slide out from the ball of yarn. With practice these movements should take only a moment.

7 Show the ball of yarn to your audience and place it in the tumbler. Take hold of the end of the yarn and pull it from the tumbler. When the yarn is completely unraveled, the coin will tinkle into the tumbler.

8 Hand the tumbler to the person from whom you borrowed the coin and ask if it is the very same coin.

# CARD CONTROL

A playing card is chosen by a spectator who then returns it to the pack. Even though the pack is thoroughly shuffled, the magician reveals the identity of the selected card in a surprising manner.

**You will need**
◊ a pack of cards

1 Shuffle the cards and then fan them out, face down, between your hands and ask someone to take any card.

2 Gather the remaining cards together and hold the pack in the left hand. As the spectator is looking at the card, lift off about two-thirds of the pack with your right hand. Ask the spectator to return the chosen card to the lower portion of the pack.

3 Replace the top portion of the cards but first place the tip of your left little finger on the chosen card. Although the pack is now reassembled, your little finger holds a "break" at the rear end of the pack.

4 Lift off about one-third of the cards immediately with your right hand and place them on the table.

5 Next lift off all the cards above your little finger and place them on top of the cards on the table.

6 Finally, place the bottom portion of the pack on top of the cards on the table. It appears that the chosen card is now completely lost in the pack but, unbeknown to the audience, it is actually the top card.

7 Pick up the pack and give it an overhand shuffle. This is a perfectly fair shuffle except for the fact that the first card is taken singly from the pack into the left hand.

8 The remaining cards are then shuffled on top of the first card. The shuffle looks perfectly normal but the chosen card is now on the bottom of the pack.

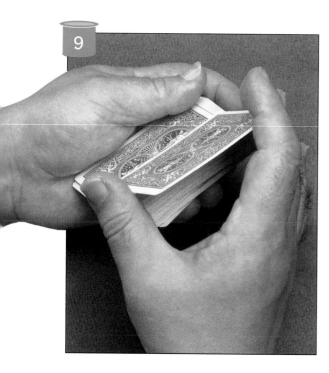

**9** Shuffle the cards again until you reach the bottom portion of the pack. As you finish the shuffle, make sure that the final part of the shuffle consists of a single card (the bottom chosen card) only. Unbeknown to the spectators, the chosen card is now back on top of the pack.

**10** As you know the location of the chosen card, there are several ways in which you can reveal its identity.

a) Fan the faces of the cards toward yourself for a brief second as if concentrating. You simply look at the top card of the pack and you can now appear to read the spectator's mind as you name the chosen card.

b) Hold the pack behind your back and say that you will try to locate the chosen card through the power of your magic fingers. Pretend to be searching through the cards and then bring forward the top card – it is the spectator's selection!

c) Ask another spectator to choose a card. But this time you do not allow a free choice – you force the top card . When both spectators are asked to name their chosen cards, they both name the same card – an amazing coincidence.

---

### TIP

• As with all tricks, you must practice this until you can do all the moves convincingly and naturally. Do not give the appearance of doing something difficult. The shuffling process must be exactly the same as you would use if you were shuffling the cards normally.

# CARD THROUGH HANDKERCHIEF

A card is selected and returned to the center of the pack. The cards are then shuffled before being wrapped in a handkerchief. When the handkerchief is shaken, one card penetrates through the fabric – it is the selected card.

**You will need**
◊ a pack of cards
◊ a handkerchief

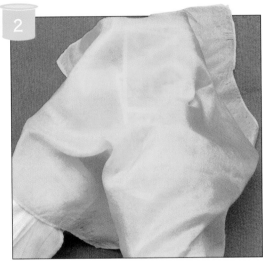

1 Have a card selected and returned to the pack. Secretly bring the chosen card to the top of the pack as described in Card Control on page 58.

2 Hold the pack in your left hand and drape the handkerchief over it. Immediately the pack is covered, your right hand reaches beneath the handkerchief, retrieves the pack, and places it on top of the fabric. Unbeknown to the audience, the top card has been left behind, resting on the palm of your left hand.

3 Grasp the edge of the handkerchief nearest your body and lift it up and forward to cover the pack.

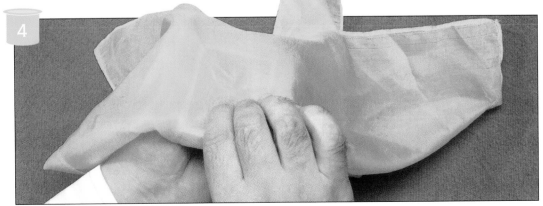

4 Your right hand now takes the pack between finger and thumb, holding it through the fabric.

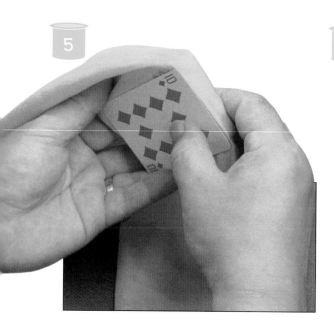

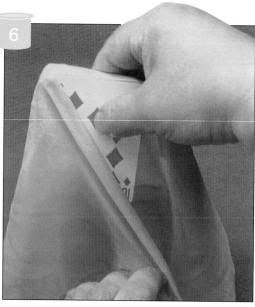

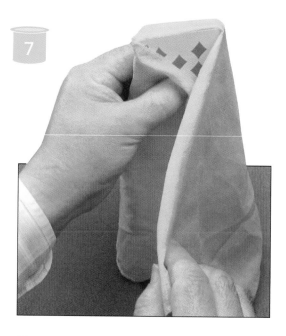

5 The selected card remains hidden beneath the handkerchief, held in position by your right thumb.

6 Your left hand now takes the left edge of the handkerchief and wraps the fabric backward and around the rear of the pack.

7 Transfer the pack (and hidden card) to your left hand, still holding it through the fabric. This leaves your right hand free to drape the right side of the fabric back and around the pack.

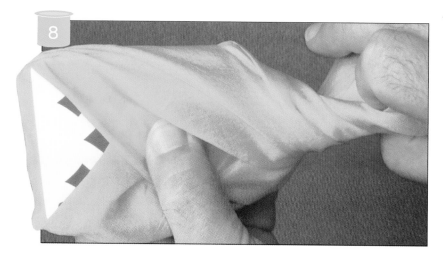

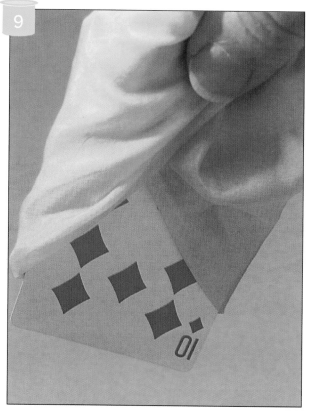

8 Take all the fabric hanging beneath the pack and twist it around several times. The pack is now completely enclosed by the fabric and the selected card is held in a pocket formed by the way the pack is wrapped. Move your right hand upward and your left down, then remove your left hand.

9 Ask the spectator to name the selected card and then begin shaking your right hand. The selected card will gradually come into view and appears to be penetrating the fabric.

# RING OFF ROPE

A finger ring is threaded onto a length of rope. Even though both ends of the rope are held by spectators, the magician manages to take the ring off the rope.

**You will need**
◊ a short length (about 1 yard) of rope or string

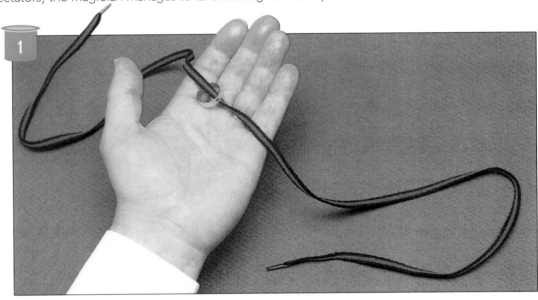

1 Ask if you can borrow a finger ring from someone in the audience. Thread the rope through the ring and display the ring on the palm of your left hand.

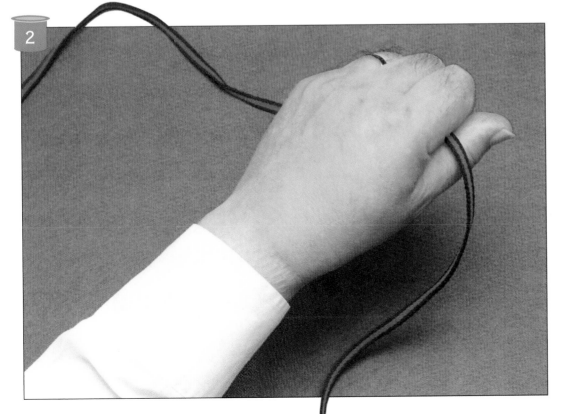

2 Close your left hand and turn it over so your fingers face the floor.

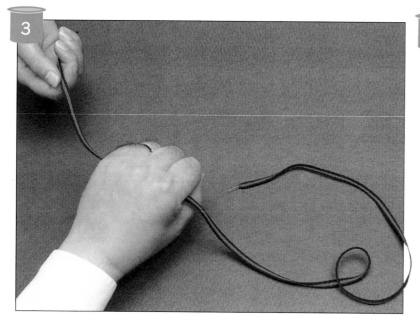

$\mathcal{3}$ As your left hand is turned over, your right hand comes in front of it and grasps the rope to the left. Your right hand continues to the left and gives the left end of the rope to a spectator to hold.

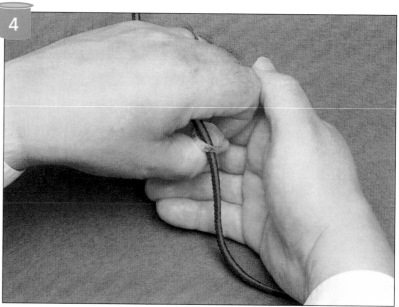

$\mathcal{4}$ Your right hand is now moved back to the right to give the right end of the rope to another spectator. It is here that the secret move that accomplishes the trick takes place. As your right hand passes beneath your left to get hold of the rope near to your left thumb, your left hand opens slightly to let the ring fall into your passing right hand.

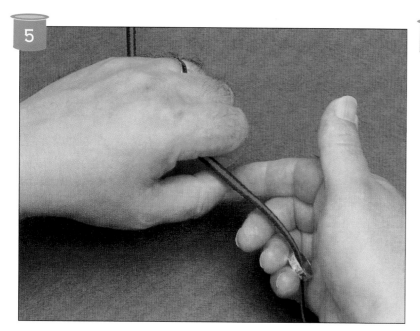

$\mathcal{5}$ Your right hand continues toward the right end of the rope with the ring concealed.

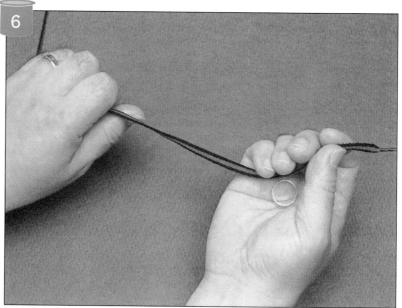

$\mathcal{6}$ Just before your right hand reaches the end of the rope, look to the spectator on the left and ask for the rope to be held slightly higher. To emphasize this, you raise your left hand. At this precise moment your right hand moves farther to the right and takes the ring off the rope.

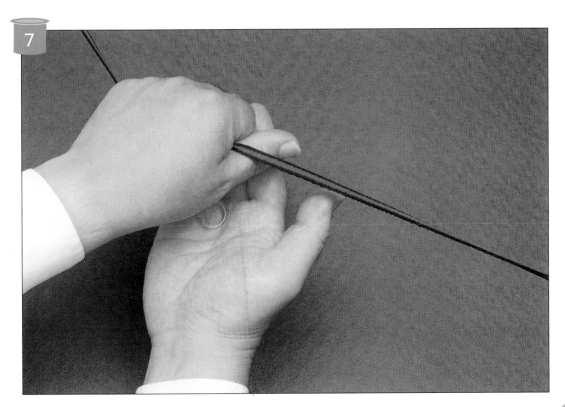

**7** Your right hand, keeping the ring hidden, then picks up the right end of the rope and gives it to someone on your right. Now both ends of the rope are being held tight by spectators. The ring is still in your right hand.

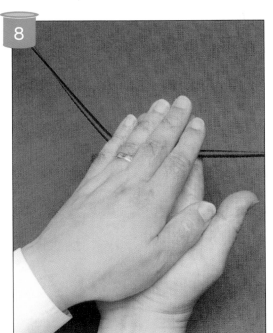

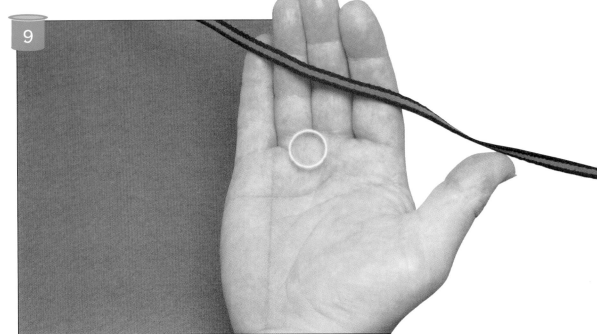

**8** Look at your left hand, which is apparently still holding the ring, and start a squeezing motion as if you are trying to maneuver the ring through the solid rope. Bring your right hand under your left and place both hands palm to palm.

**9** Roll your palms together for a moment and then lift your left hand to reveal the ring on your right. It seems that the ring has penetrated the rope.

# RING ON PENCIL

A finger ring, borrowed from a spectator, vanishes and reappears on the center of a pencil.

**You will need**
◊ a special "vanishing" handkerchief
◊ a paper bag
◊ a long pencil

1 To make the special handkerchief required for this trick, you will need, in addition to the handkerchief itself, a piece of matching fabric, a metal ring, and needle and thread.

Cut a small triangle from the extra fabric and sew it onto one corner of the handkerchief. Before sewing up the third side, place the ring in the pocket you have formed. Sew up the third side to enclose the ring and your preparation is complete.

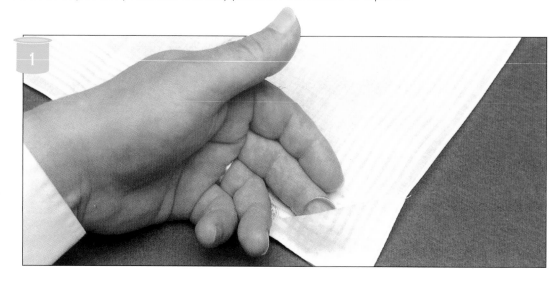

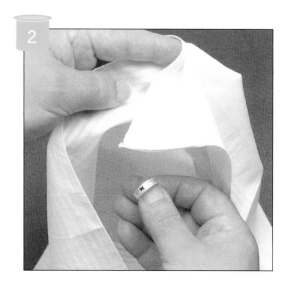

2 In performance you first borrow a finger ring from a member of the audience. Hold the ring between the thumb and first finger of your left hand and then drape the handkerchief over it.

3 You now hand the handkerchief to a second person with the request that he or she guard it safely. In actual fact you now have the ring in your possession. This is how you get it. As you approach the second spectator, your right hand takes the corner of the handkerchief containing the secret ring and puts it up into your left fingers. At the same time the borrowed ring is allowed to drop from your left hand into the right.

4 Hand the handkerchief to the second spectator, asking him or her to keep hold of the ring. In fact it is the secret ring that the spectator is holding. This is the reason why you do not use the owner of the ring for this part of the trick as he or she might determine by touch that the ring in the handkerchief is not his or her own ring.

| TIP |
| --- |
| • A similar handkerchief with a coin in the pocket can be used to make a coin disappear. |

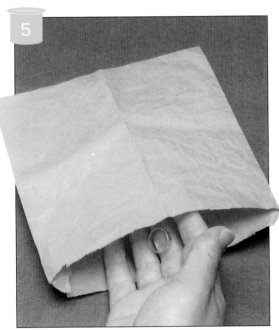

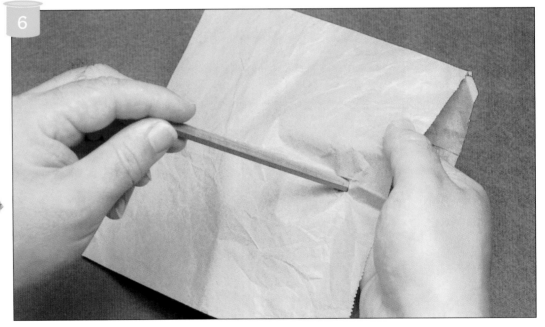

5 With your right hand concealing the ring, reach over to the paper bag that is lying on your table. Do this naturally and casually and do not look at your right hand as you do this. If you look at your hand, you will draw attention to it and this could arouse suspicions in the minds of the audience. Try to forget the fact that you have a ring in your hand. If you start worrying about it, you could transmit your unease and that would spoil the effect.

6 Holding the bag in your right hand, reach in with your left to take out the pencil. In a subtle way this "proves" that the bag is otherwise empty. Do not mention the fact that the bag is empty, because by doing so you would only draw attention to it.

Now push the pencil through one side of the bag and out the other. In so doing, you push the pencil through the hidden ring. Remove your right hand from the bag and screw up the top of the bag.

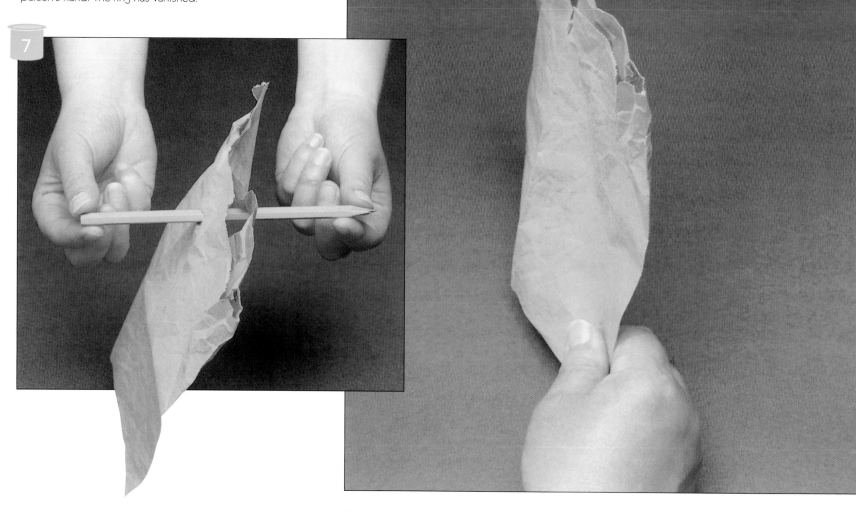

7 Hand the pencil to the spectator from whom you borrowed the ring with the request that he or she holds each end of it. Go back to the second spectator who is still holding the handkerchief. Take one corner of the handkerchief and pull it from the person's hand. The ring has vanished!

8 Go back to the first person and pull the bag downward to reveal the ring on the center of the pencil. Ask the owner to confirm that it is indeed his or her ring and thank both of your assistants for their help.

# THE COIN FOLD

A coin is wrapped in a piece of paper from where it disappears.

**You will need**
◊ a coin
◊ a square sheet of paper

1 This is a superb trick to perform on the spur of the moment for the coin can be borrowed and the paper can be simply a square torn from a newspaper (or whatever else is available). Place the coin on the center of the square of paper.

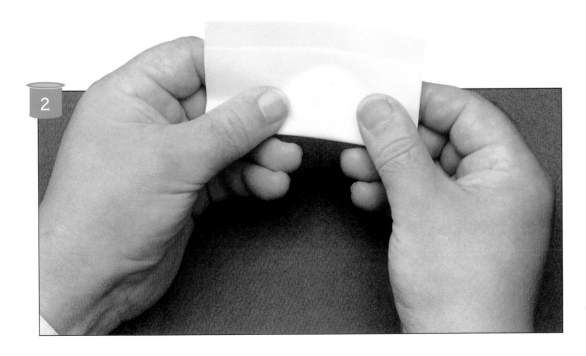

2 Fold the bottom edge of the paper up and over the coin. Do not bring the bottom edge right up to meet the top edge but about ¾ inch below it.

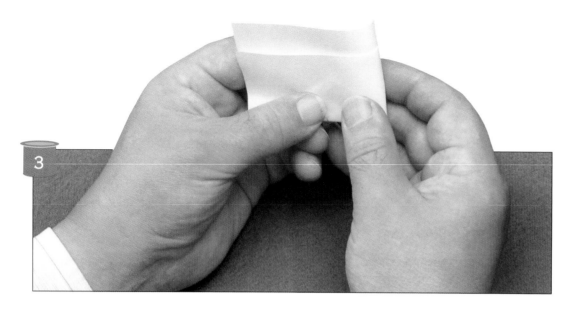

3 Fold the right edge of the paper back behind
the coin.

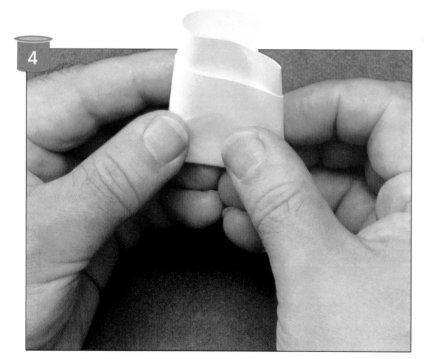

4 Fold the left edge back and behind the coin.

5 For the final fold, bend the top flap of paper back
behind the coin. It appears that the coin is secure in the
paper but in fact the top edge is open.

6 Turn the paper around so that the open edge is toward the bottom. The coin can now slip from its paper prison into your right hand.

7 Tear up the paper and throw the pieces on the table. The coin has apparently vanished but, in reality, remains concealed in your right hand.

# A CAPITAL PREDICTION

The performer shows a bag containing numerous slips of paper on which are written the names of capital cities. Some of the slips are removed from the bag and the names called out to give some indication of the range available. Finally, one slip is withdrawn from the bag and the chosen capital named. A large envelope, which has been on view throughout, is then opened to reveal a card bearing the name of the chosen city.

**You will need**
◊ a change bag (a utility prop that can be used for hundreds of tricks)
◊ about 100 slips of paper measuring approximately 3 x 1¼ inches
◊ ball-point pen or typewriter
◊ a piece of card
◊ a large envelope

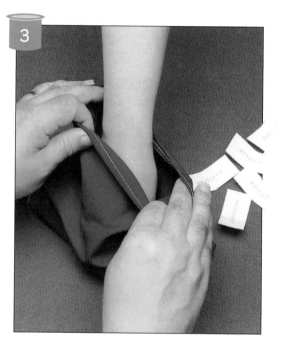

1 A change bag is simply a cloth bag in which there is a central divider. As the audience is not aware of this, it is possible to put something into the bag (putting it into one of the compartments) and then show the bag empty (by showing the other compartment). The easiest way to make such a bag is to take a strip of fabric measuring approximately 20 x 8 inches. Fold the fabric into three and then sew down the sides and bottom to make the bag. An even simpler change bag can be made by gluing two paper bags together.

2 On 50 slips of paper write the name of one capital city. Let's use Paris as an example. Fold these slips of paper in half and drop all into one side of your bag. Write the names of different capital cities on each of the remaining 50 slips. Fold these in half and place them in the other compartment of the bag. Write the name Paris on the card, place this in the large envelope, and you are ready to perform.

3 Show the envelope to the audience and place it in a position where it can be observed by them. Pick up the change bag, reach into the compartment with the different cities and pull out a handful of slips. Let them fall from your fingers and then let them fall back into the bag as you say, "I have here over a hundred [magic is all about lying] slips of paper bearing the names of capital cities and I would like one of them to be chosen." Invite someone up to assist you and ask that person to draw out a few slips from the bag, unfold them and call out the names of the cities written on them.

### TIP

• There are literally hundreds of tricks that can be done with a change bag: three colored handkerchiefs, dropped into the bag, become knotted together; a sheet of paper torn into pieces and dropped into the bag is magically restored; a long piece of rope is dropped into the bag and when it is removed, there are lots of knots along its length; and many, many more.

4 You now explain that this time you want just one slip to be taken. While you are talking, alter the positions of your fingers on the bag so that next time you open it, the spectator reaches into the other compartment (the one in which all the slips bear the same name).

5 One slip is chosen and the name read out (it is, of course, Paris). Emphasize that the spectator had a perfectly free choice (another lie) and draw attention to the envelope that has been on view throughout.

6 When the envelope is opened, it is seen that you accurately predicted which capital city would be chosen.

# DRINK FROM NOWHERE

A handkerchief is shown on both sides and then draped over the magician's hand. Suddenly, a form appears beneath the fabric. When the handkerchief is removed, there, standing on the magician's hand, is a wineglass – full of wine!

**You will need**
◊ some wine, fruit juice, or other liquid
◊ a wineglass
◊ a sheet of strong kitchen wrap (large enough to cover the mouth of the glass)
◊ an elastic band
◊ a handkerchief

1 Pour the liquid into the glass and cover the glass with the kitchen wrap. Use the elastic band to hold the wrap in place. The elastic band must be tight enough to hold the wrap securely but with sufficient elasticity to enable you to remove it easily without fumbling. You will have to experiment to find the right band for the glass you are using.

2 Now place the glass in your left armpit, with the bottom of the glass facing the audience. Adjust the fabric of your clothing to cover as much of the base as possible. Because of this positioning of the glass, this trick has to be the opening one in your performance.

3 Walk onto the stage and display the handkechief between your hands.

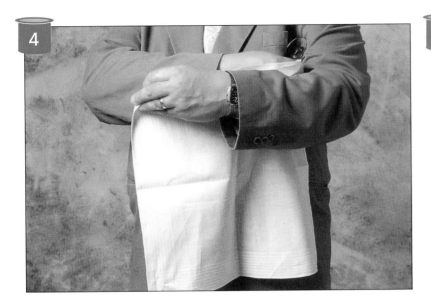

4 Now bring your left hand forward and to the right as your right hand moves to the left. This movement lets you show the other side of the handkerchief. It also brings your right hand in the correct position to "steal" the glass from its hiding place.

5 Grip the stem of the glass between the second and third fingers of your right hand and then move your hands back to their opening position, with the handkerchief spread out between them. The glass is now hidden behind the top right corner of the handkerchief.

6 Let go of the right corner as your right hand moves to the center of the material. At the same time use your left hand to smooth the fabric out over your right palm. Because the glass is still hanging from your fingers, there is no indication that anything has happened.

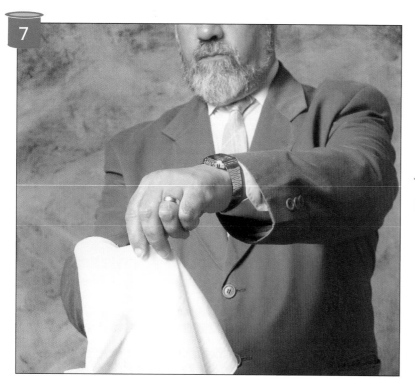

$7$ Your left fingers now grip the center of the handkerchief and lift it upward. At the same time your right hand swivels the glass into an upright position.

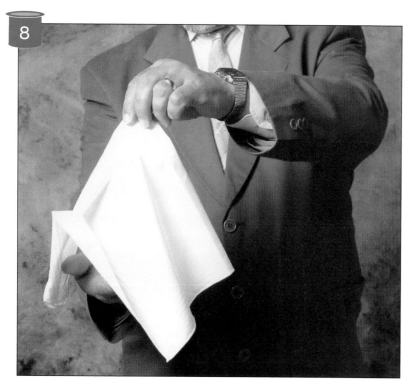

$8$ Your left hand is now lowered and the fact that something has appeared beneath the handkerchief is immediately apparent to the audience.

$9$ Your left fingers, working through the fabric, pull the elastic band and cover off the glass, and then pull the handkerchief away. The glass is revealed and while attention is on this, put the handkerchief, with the cover and band hidden inside, quickly to one side.

# THE RISING CARDS

This is one of the classics of magic – three chosen cards rise from the pack of their own accord.

**You will need**
◊ a pack of cards
◊ razor blade or sharp knife
◊ about 1 yard of fine black thread
◊ a glass tumbler that will hold a
   pack of cards
◊ a small tray

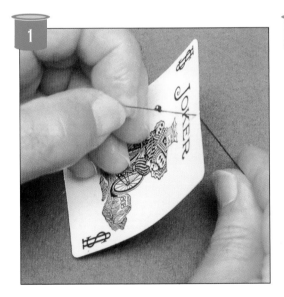

1 Take one card and cut a slit in one end of it using a razor blade or sharp knife. Push one end of the cotton through the slits and tie several knots in the end.

2 Place one card face down on your table and the prepared card face down on top of it. The slit in the prepared card should be facing toward the back of the table. The thread hangs down from the card onto the floor. The tumbler and the rest of the pack are in front of the face-down cards.

3 When you wish to do the trick, pick up the pack and give the cards a shuffle. Ask three spectators each to take a card. They keep their cards while you return to your table. Place the pack down on top of the two cards already there.

4 Pick up the glass and show it to the audience. Put the glass back on the table and pick up the pack. Place the pack in the glass in such a way that the thread runs from the front of the pack, across the top of the cards, and then down to the floor.

5 Collect the chosen cards on the tray and then place them, one by one, into the pack. This action pushes the thread down to the bottom of the pack.

6 Place your foot on the thread on the floor (it may help to stick a small pellet of paper to the end of the thread to enable you to spot it more easily). Lift up the glass and ask for the names of the three cards. As the glass is lifted, the thread is tautened and the cards will rise from the pack one by one.

# ON THE TIP OF MY TONGUE

A comedy card trick. The magician tries some mind-reading and fails . . . but not for long.

**You will need**
◊ a pack of cards
◊ a piece of paper upon which is written "six of clubs"
◊ a handkerchief

1 Put the six of clubs (or whichever card you decide to use) on the bottom of the pack. Put the pack and the handkerchief on the table. Hide the piece of paper in some place where you can retrieve it easily without anyone noticing.

2 Pick up the pack with your right hand and cover it with the handkerchief. As you are arranging the fabric of the handkerchief, use your right fingers to pull the bottom card slightly to one side. (For the sake of clarity the handkerchief has been removed in the photographs.)

3 You then say that you want someone to lift off a portion of cards through the fabric and then to reach beneath the handkerchief and take the next card from the pack. You demonstrate this by lifting off some cards but in fact you actually lift all the cards except the bottom one. (This is quite easy to do because the bottom card is out of alignment.)

4 This lets you turn the bottom card, which is still on your left hand, face up.

5 Put the pack together again and let the spectator lift off some cards. As soon as this is done, you secretly turn the bottom half over.

6 When the spectator reaches beneath the handkerchief to take the "next" card, it is the reversed card that is taken.

**7**

**7** As soon as the card has been taken, turn the bottom half of the pack back the right way and let the spectator replace the top half. It appears that the spectator has had a free choice of card but the card has actually been "forced."

**8**

**8** Place the pack and handkerchief back down on the table and ask the spectator to show the chosen card to the rest of the audience. While all attention is on this action, retrieve the piece of paper and put it in your mouth. Rest it on your tongue.

**9** Announce that you will now read the spectator's mind and will reveal the name of the chosen card. You then make a few inaccurate guesses as to the identity of the card. Annoyed at this lack of success, you say, "I don't know what's wrong with me today. A second ago I had the name of your card on the tip of my tongue." As you say this, put out your tongue to reveal the paper. Take the paper from your mouth and show the writing – you really did have the spectator's card on the tip of your tongue!

**9**

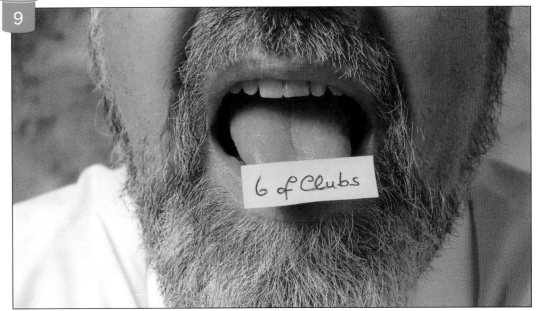

# SUN AND MOON

Two squares of paper, one red and one yellow, have their centers removed. The magician restores them but the red center is now in the yellow square and the yellow center is in the red square. The magician's powers are once again conjured up and this time the two squares of paper are restored correctly.

**You will need**
◊ a card template, ⅛ of a circle
◊ four squares of red paper
◊ four squares of yellow paper
◊ scissors
◊ glue
◊ paper clip
◊ a change bag (as described on page 24)

1 Fold one square of each color in half lengthways then widthways to form a smaller square. Fold this diagonally to give a triangle. Use the template to cut a circle from each triangle. For descriptive purposes we will call the cutout circles R1 (for red) and Y1 (for yellow). Keep the circles and discard the rest of each square.

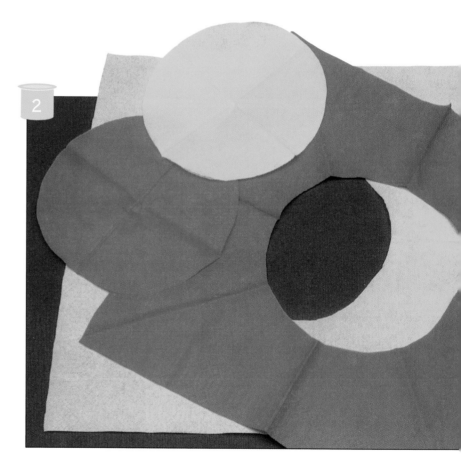

2 Cut two slightly smaller circles from the centers of two other squares of paper (again, one red and one yellow). Discard the circles you have cut out and then glue R1 onto the hole in the yellow square and Y1 onto the hole in the red square. You now have a yellow square with a red circle in its center and a red square with a yellow circle in its center.

3 When the glue has dried, fold the two prepared squares into four and put a paper clip over them. Now put them in the front compartment of a change bag. Alongside them, place two ordinary squares (one red and one yellow) similarly folded. The two remaining squares are also folded into four and placed on your table. Before placing the squares on the table, draw part of a circle in pencil on their centers (using the same card template you used earlier). You are now ready to perform. Pick up the squares from the table and display them. Now use the scissors to cut a circle from the center of each paper (use your penciled guidelines to get the cutting more or less the right size).

4 Show the two squares with the holes in them and then show the two paper circles. Fold them all up and put them into the back pocket of the change bag. Say a few magic words and then place your hand in the front compartment of the bag. Find the papers with the paper clip, pull off the clip, and bring them into view.

5 You claim to have restored the papers but when they are unfolded, it seems you have gone terribly wrong – the yellow paper has a red circle in its center and the red a yellow circle.

6 Fold up the faulty papers (or tear them up first if you wish) and put them into the rear compartment of the change bag.

7 This time you use some stronger magic words before reaching into the front compartment of the bag to remove the papers therein. Open out the papers and they are seen to be fully restored – another miracle accomplished!

# SOLID THROUGH SOLID

Two colored handkerchiefs are wrapped around one another until it is absolutely impossible for them to be parted. The magician blows on them and the handkerchiefs appear to melt through one another.

**You will need**
◊ two colored handkerchiefs

1 For the purposes of description we will assume that one handkerchief is purple and the other is red, although the actual colors are immaterial. Take the diagonally opposite corners of each handkerchief and roll the fabric into a tube shape. Place the purple handkerchief on the table and then lay the red one across it at 90 degrees.

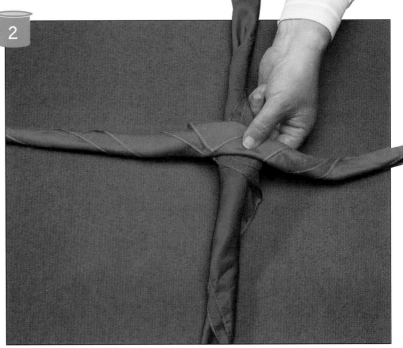

2 Pick up the handkerchiefs where they cross between the thumb and fingers of your hand.

$3$ Your right hand now approaches from the right and goes beneath the purple handkerchief to take hold the left end of the red handkerchief.

$4$ This end is then taken to the right, below the purple handkerchief and then back to the left over the top of the purple.

$5$ Now take the nearest end of the purple handkerchief below and then back over the red.

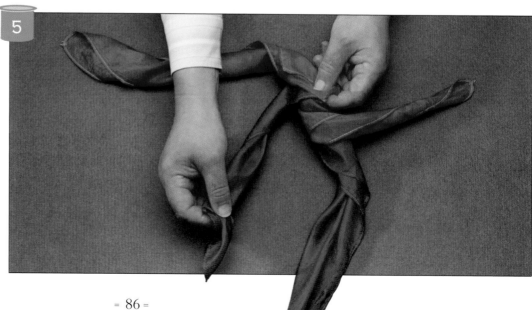

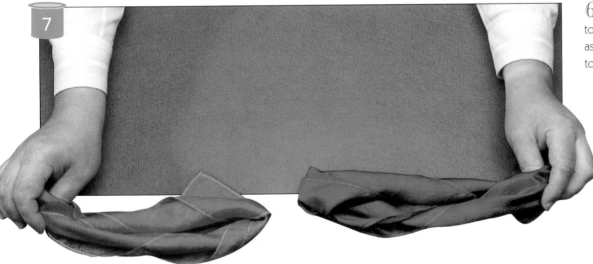

6 Hold the two ends of the red handkerchief together and the two purple ends together. It looks as if the handkerchiefs are inextricably locked together.

7 Blow gently on the handkerchiefs (to make the magic work) and then pull your hands apart. Amazingly, the two handkerchiefs separate!

# CUT AND RESTORED ROPE

A length of rope is cut into two pieces and then restored to one by the magician.

**You will need**
◊ a small piece of rope
◊ transparent adhesive tape
◊ a good length of rope
◊ a handkerchief
◊ scissors

1 Take the smaller piece of rope and form it into a small loop using the tape to hold the join. Place the loop over the long piece of rope and lay both on your table, using the handkerchief or something else to conceal the ring from the spectators' view. In performance you pick up the rope with your right hand. Your hand actually goes around the loop.

2 Take the bottom end of the rope in your left hand and hold the rope between your hands. (This gives the audience the impression that you are holding a single length of rope – they have no knowledge of the loop of rope concealed by the fingers of your right hand.)

3 Lift your left hand upward toward the end of the rope held in your right hand. Your left hand now grasps the end above your right hand and your right hand moves down to the center of the rope (taking the hidden loop with it). Let go of the rope ends held in your left hand as your right hand moves upward (apparently to show the center of the rope but by this time part of the loop has been allowed to come into view).

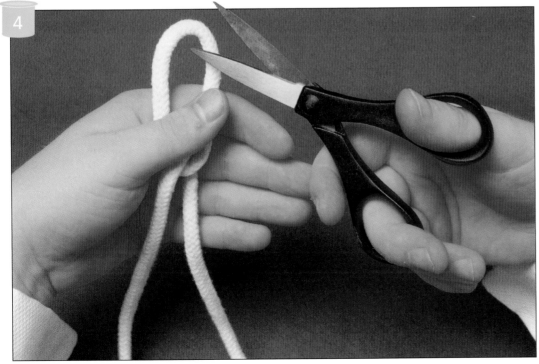

4 Transfer what appears to be the center of the rope from your right hand into your left (being careful not to reveal the loop). Do not make anything special of this movement. It should appear that you have simply transferred the center of the rope from one hand to the other so that you can pick up the scissors with your right hand. Take the scissors in your right hand and apparently cut through the center of the rope (in fact you are just cutting through the extra loop of rope).

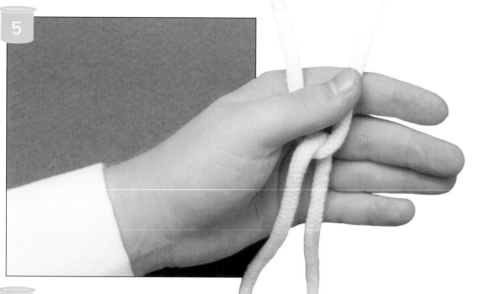

**5** It now appears that you have two pieces of rope in your hand because the spectators can see two ends above your left hand and two ends at the lower position.

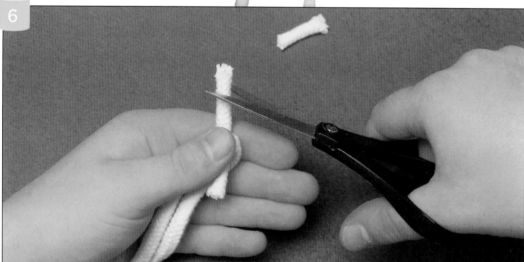

**6** Use the scissors to "trim" the top ends (but actually you trim off so much that you cut away all of the secret loop).

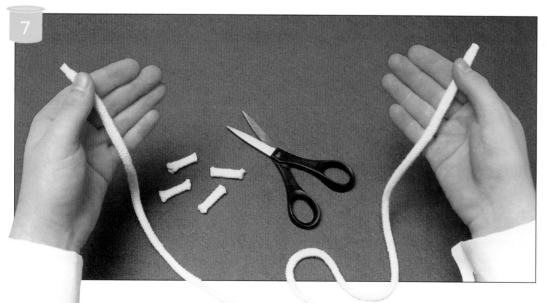

**7** Put the scissors down. Wave your right hand over the "cut" center of the rope. Bring both hands out to the ends of the rope and show the completely restored rope as you take your bow.

# BANK NIGHT

Four envelopes numbered 1 to 4 are shown. The magician explains that one of them contains some money and that three lucky people will be given the chance to win it. Three envelopes are chosen by spectators, leaving the magician with just one. When the spectators open their envelopes they are seen to be unlucky. The magician opens the remaining, unchosen envelope, and wins the cash!

**You will need**

◊ four numbered envelopes
◊ a large denomination bill
◊ four pieces of paper the same size as the bill

$1$ Before your performance place a piece of paper in each envelope. Seal the envelopes and number them 1 to 4. The numbering can be done with a pen, be printed, or use numbered gummed stickers available from most stationers.

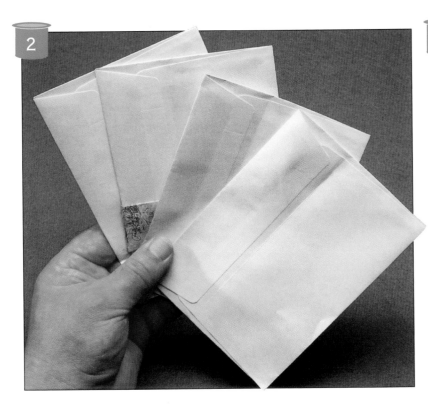

$2$ Place the envelopes in a fan shape (in numerical order) on your table, envelope number 1 being to the left of the fan. Fold the bill into four and slip it onto the left edge of envelope number 2. Now turn all the envelopes over to conceal the bill beneath them.

$3$ In performance pick up the envelopes between your left thumb and forefinger and turn them so that the numbers are facing the audience. The concealed bill will be visible to you but hidden from the audience's view.

4 You now let each of three spectators select an envelope by calling out its number. Whichever number is chosen, you pull it from the fan and hand it to the spectator. It is important that you keep the bill concealed behind the fingers of your left hand as you do this.

5 When you are left with just one envelope, hold it with the bill still hidden behind it.

6 Ask the spectators if they wish to change their envelopes. They can exchange with one another or they can exchange with you. If they exchange with one another, you have nothing to worry about. If someone wants to exchange with you, take their envelope and place it in front of the envelope you hold. Then remove your envelope and hand it to the spectator. In this way the bill remains hidden at all times.

7 Ask the spectators to open their envelopes to see if they have won – unfortunately, they have not! Keeping then bill hidden, begin to open your envelope.

8 Place your right fingers into your envelope. Your thumb goes behind the envelope and onto the bill. Now move your hand to the right, pulling the note to the right with your thumb.

### TIP

• Instead of leaving the envelopes empty, each could contain a little note of consolation which each spectator is asked to read out. Suitable phrases include "Money isn't everything," "You can't win them all," "Better luck next time," and so on. If you can come up with some amusing phrases, so much the better as this will add a little light comedy to the proceedings.

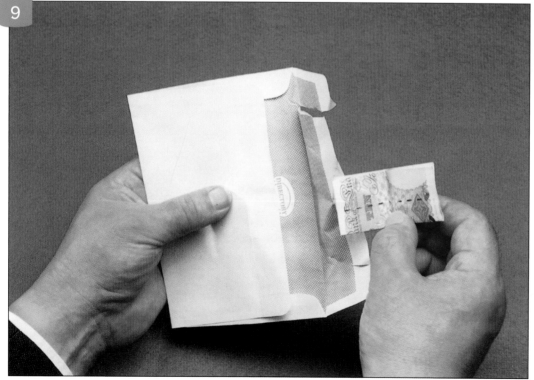

9 As your fingers clear the envelope, the bill, held between fingers and thumb, becomes visible to the audience. The illusion of it coming from the envelope is absolutely perfect – and you appear to have won the money!

# SEE-THROUGH PRODUCTION

A box is shown completely empty, then the magician proceeds to produce a variety of handkerchiefs and colored streamers from it.

**You will need**
◊ a square box with an open front
◊ a tube glued inside the box
◊ a square tube (small enough to fit into the box but large enough to go over the fixed tube)
◊ silk scarves, ribbons, paper streamers, etc.

1 Put the ribbons, streamers, or whatever else is to be produced into the inner tube. Place the square tube into the box.

2 In performance you just lift out the square tube and show it to be empty. At this point, although you must not draw attention to the fact, the audience can see through the cutout in the front of the box. Because the interior is black and the inner tube is also black, it seems that the box is empty.

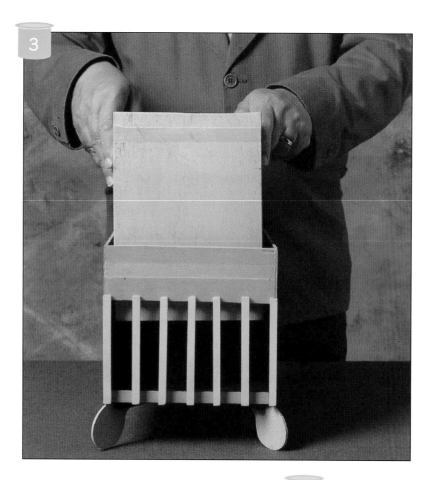

3 Place the square tube back in position.

4 Wave your hands over the boxes in a mystical manner and then reach in to produce the scarves, handkerchiefs, colored streamers and so on.